Ballads, Blues & Swan Songs

Books by William Wiser

BALLADS, BLUES & SWAN SONGS

William Wiser

Atheneum   1982   New York

These stories first appeared in *Antioch Review, The Carleton Miscellany, Cosmopolitan, Encounter, Georgia Review, Kenyon Review, Massachusetts Review, Playboy,* and *Southern Review.*

Library of Congress Cataloging in Publication Data

Wiser, William.
Ballads, blues & swan songs.

Contents: Country music—The man who wrote letters to presidents—A soliloquy in tongues [etc.]
I. Title.
PS3573.I87B3   1982   813'54   81-66032
ISBN 0-689-11188-6   AACR2

Copyright © 1964, 1965, 1966, 1967, 1971, 1973, 1974, 1976, 1982
by William Wiser
All rights reserved
Published simultaneously in Canada by McClelland and Stewart Ltd.
Composed by American–Stratford Graphic Services,
Brattleboro, Vermont
Manufactured by American Book–Stratford Press,
Saddle Brook, New Jersey
Designed by Mary Cregan
First Edition

For my mother

Contents

Ballads, Blues & Swan Songs

Country Music

FOR A LONG TIME the navy would not let Negroes be anything but steward mates: they served as messboys in the officers' wardroom, or worked in the ship's laundry. All of that has changed. Many are now in engineering divisions—or gunnery, or fire control. There is only one black sailor aboard the USS *Halstead;* his name is Littlejohn, and he is striking for quartermaster.

During working hours Littlejohn mostly chips paint with the deck force, for they are shorthanded, but as a quartermaster striker he has been taught the points of the compass and the difference between cirrus and cirrocumulus clouds. Tonight he is in the wheelhouse standing midwatch as messenger to Mister Walker, officer of the watch

—allowed to make coffee and wear a pair of earphones. From time to time the forward lookout reports a light on the horizon, and Littlejohn relays the bearing to Mister Walker.

Midwatch is said to be the longest and lonesomest watch aboard ship. You think it will never end. Sailors swap tales to make the time pass: tales of girls they have known, and invariably bedded; monumental drinking bouts they have staged in some foreign port—adventures they have had (or might have had) at sea and ashore. These tales are known as sea stories, and you can believe them or not. A sailor's yarn—no matter how exaggerated or farfetched —makes the monotonous hours of the long watch pass. Littlejohn listens to every tale they have to tell, but he has never told one of his own. He is new to the ship and not long in the navy; if he told a sea story he might tell about the time a white woman drove him all around Copper Basin County, in a red car, and made him sit in the front seat and bought a pistol from him for twenty-five dollars— which is just as unlikely as most of the tales he has heard. But there is no point to that story, nor any ending to it, so he does not tell it.

Finally, at 0330, Littlejohn will go around the ship waking sailors who are on the watch list for the four-to-eight relief.

"Hey, Littlejohn," says the helmsman, "play us something, why don't you?"

Littlejohn keeps a harmonica down in the flag bag, and plays sometimes.

"We are on radio silence," says Mister Walker.

The ship is bound for Vieques, in Puerto Rico, where a mock invasion of marines will be acted out. It is a simulated wartime operation, and the ship is on practice radio silence every other night.

4

"He's not going to go on the radio, sir," says Bailey, QM 1, Littlejohn's division PO.

"You'd be surprised how sound travels across water," says Mister Walker, who is fresh out of Annapolis.

All his life Littlejohn has found himself between white men wanting him to do something different.

"He'll play soft," says the helmsman, "sir."

The helmsman is from South Carolina, and favors country music. There are a good many southern boys aboard the *Halstead,* and Littlejohn knows how to play the music they like. With his harmonica he can mimic everything from a yodel to a death rattle—Nashville style, West Texas, or what-have-you. Also, Littlejohn knows how to read music, if need be—taught to him by a white man named Lionel, accompanist to concert stars, in the place where Littlejohn grew up. Littlejohn knows a lot more music than the southern boys suspect, but on board the *Halstead* he plays country music.

"Permission granted," says Mister Walker, who is a stickler for terminology and has learned at Annapolis not to alienate your enlisted man.

Littlejohn gives his headset to the relief helmsman and goes out to the signal bridge to get his harmonica out of the flag bag.

As soon as he is back, the helmsman asks for "Who Was That Dude I Saw You With Last Night?" but Bailey wants him to play "The Sincerest Story Ever Told."

When you cannot please everybody, a white man named Trace once told him (he was a drinking man, and took a drink whenever he felt like it), you might as well please yourself. All his life Littlejohn has been at the beck and call of whites, and they are always calling out opposite orders. Littlejohn has just learned that there are thirty-two points on the mariner's compass, divided into three hundred and sixty degrees, and he believes he has traveled every one of those directions trying to get along and do what whites want. Only just lately was he getting to where he wanted to go his own way for a change.

What he would do, he would play them some music that wasn't one tune or the other, a song of his own he made up himself. They will not know the difference. The song is called "Nigger Don't Let the Sun Set on Your Head in Copper Basin County," but naturally he does not give out the name of the piece he is about to play. It is all country music to them.

"Wearing a sailor suit so white it like to put your eyes out," was the way a taxi driver told it, when Franklin stepped off the Smoky Mountains Trailways bus in Watershed after nearly two years away.

Not that people around town recognized him. Negroes are rare in this part of Tennessee, but a black boy growing up here goes mostly unnoticed—the white sailor suit was what caught people's attention. But Franklin knew them. Just about every face was a familiar one—even if he could not put a name to it—and he stepped off the bus with a fearful heart to see this same street again, with the same people walking it. He was perspiring to beat the band under his white navy hat, but too scared to take it off and cool himself. The hat represented the government. It was a protection against those farmers leaning out of pickup trucks and their women, coming out of the drugstore, with faces fierce as turkeys, and big strapping country boys lounging around town. The hat was a badge that said Franklin belonged to the navy now—was government property, in fact—and Watershed had best leave him be.

Franklin had a set of leave papers in his canvas bag, allowing him nine days' leave before his ship got under way, along with the return half of a round-trip ticket to Norfolk. He carried a harmonica in the front pocket of his jumper; sailors generally carry their cigarettes there, but Franklin did not smoke. He touched the harmonica out of nervousness and picked up his bag and started down Depot Street to the part of town known as Summit. He gritted his teeth and fastened his eyes straight ahead, fixed on some invisible spot not even Franklin could see. He had made up his mind not to step off the sidewalk and walk in the gutter as he used to do when he was little. Folks did seem to make a path for him, as if following some maritime law of right-of-way.

Then, when he heard somebody behind him say, "I swear if that ain't the Tolliver nigger," it felt like a shotgun aimed at the back of his neck. But he walked on, and the only threat made was a spotted hound that ran out of the barbershop to bark at him—but in a foolish way, and more at the uniform than at Franklin.

That was something a black boy always had to watch out for: people's dogs. Trace would send him to the mineral spring for pure water to drink his whiskey with (for the city water tastes of copper), and there were mean dogs along that path. Franklin had been bitten more than once. Poor whites in cabins with an icebox on the porch to show they were not *that* poor, lived out toward the spring, and they all kept dogs. Try and get a white man to call off his dog, if you are black—they think it is good sport. Franklin was obliged to search out devious back ways when going for water, and carry a stick.

Passing the Baptist church was where Franklin's hands and feet turned cold, hot as it was. He was remembering Billie Jean Ellis, who used to play piano for the church choir—did she still? The deacons were outraged at her low-neck dresses at choir practice—or said they were—

and the BTU did not know whether to believe half the stories they heard about her or not. But she was a star piano player, so the church put up with her.

Franklin had worked part-time at the church, too—doing odd jobs for pocket money. He remembered sitting on the parsonage steps once, playing his harmonica. The preacher came out and saw him and said, "That's right, son, make a joyful noise unto the Lord." Nobody had ever called him son before. He tried to like the preacher after that, though he had never been allowed to attend a church service or step inside the church of a Sunday— only weekdays, to do the floors and polish pews and carry last Sunday's dead flowers off the altar. The preacher's wife once gave him a cold leftover waffle she said "would only go to waste," and stood by to watch him eat it.

Another time he came within an inch of getting bit by a black widow spider, pulling up a rotted-out stump, out front of the church. Here he was thinking about Billie Jean Ellis and a black widow spider at the same time, feeling cold all over.

Watershed was built on the side of a hill and every street lengthwise, from city limit to cemetery, was higher than the one before. The connecting streets ran up and down hill at a steep angle. Franklin climbed one of these, called Grandview Drive, to get to Summit by a back way. Grandview had no particular grand view till you got to the end of it, at the highest part of town, and even then all you saw was flat tar roofs in the downtown part of Watershed, the brick backside of the bank (the front was marble), and the top of the courthouse with a flag flying. The hills beyond were not worth looking at, for that was the direction of the copper mines, and nothing grew there.

Franklin recalled that this was the way he had followed Laudermilk home that time. One evening Franklin took it into his head to follow the beggar man. (This reminded him he might have been followed, himself, and he searched Grandview Drive for a shadow—but the only soul in sight was Mister Culpepper, of Harmony Hardware, out sprinkling his lawn.) Franklin then looked out over the town with a sigh. He felt a lot easier about being this high up, as if the town could not get at him, away up here.

"Howdy, sailor," said Mister Culpepper, who was commander of the American Legion Post in Watershed and took an interest in things military.

"How do, Mister Culpepper."

Mister Culpepper was startled to hear himself called by name by a black sailor he did not know from Adam. He almost sprinkled his shoetops, squinting and trying to figure out who Franklin could be.

When Franklin followed Laudermilk home that time he went slow about it, for the beggar's legs were cut off at the hip, and he had to navigate the streets on a wooden platform with roller-skate wheels nailed to it, pushing himself along with railroad gloves. Laudermilk played a mouth organ on Saturdays in front of the Five and Dime downtown. He kept his cap laid out upside down on the street curb beside him for people to drop money into. Weekdays he went from house to house on his little roller-skate platform, where charity-minded church ladies saved bread and beans and bacon grease for him.

It was said that Laudermilk slept in that old cracked-open mausoleum in the cemetery with MOWBERRY carved into the marble. The Lions Club had a meeting about it, and somebody put in a motion to investigate. The mayor was pressured to send Mister Stiles, the jailor, to evict Laudermilk from the cemetery (if he really did sleep there), but Mister Stiles never got around to it—anyway, Laudermilk was a pitiful cripple, and there were no living descendants of the Mowberrys to file a complaint.

Franklin had always been halfway afraid of the beggar
—there was something fierce in the set of Laudermilk's
mouth—but he dearly wanted to hear that harmonica up
close. Sometimes at night you could hear mouth-organ
music coming out of the cemetery. In town, Franklin
knew better than to linger too long in front of the Five
and Dime where Laudermilk played. White people would
not tolerate a black boy hanging around a place where
they congregated. So he decided to follow Laudermilk
home and listen to him from somewhere out of sight, in
the cemetery.

Franklin was only nine then, and Grandview Drive
was steeper than it is now. Also, back then, it was tar
sprinkled with gravel instead of hardtop concrete. The
way Laudermilk dealt with it was to crisscross all the way
up, like a spider working a web. He used his arms as a
kind of catapult, so as to hop right over patches of gravel
that were too loose and slippery to roll over with a roller-
skate platform. He was a young fellow, for a beggar, with
a big chest and thick arms from pushing himself along on
a platform all his life. Franklin followed from a considerable distance, but crisscrossed Grandview the very same
way Laudermilk did.

Now, as Franklin came to the path that ran between
the new cemetery and the old, he saw himself the way he
was back then, scrambling up the hillside drive to try and
sneak up on a crippled harmonica player, to hear him
play. A circle of gnats spun around his white hat where
he had been sweating, so he stopped and took his hat off
and wiped his head with a white handkerchief from the
canvas bag. From this side of Summit he could see the old
Copper Basin lumber mill, about to fall down, that went
out of business. Next to the railroad siding where the lumber used to be stacked was a brand-new Big Dixie supermarket. You could see the courthouse in the center of

everything, made out of Tennessee marble from a quarry not ten miles away. In fact, marble was so plentiful around the county that folks used it for porch steps instead of wood or cement, and even little cabins out in the hills—with weatherbeaten shingles blown apart like a deck of cards—had marble porch steps. One, that Franklin knew of, on the path to the mineral spring, even had a marble drinking trough for livestock.

Behind the courthouse was the jail, with a marble front but cinder block in back. That was where Trace had set up his dental office, with all his equipment, and where you had to go to get your teeth fixed. At first it was a joke, but folks around town finally got used to it and by and by thought nothing of it. People will get used to anything. Look at how Franklin had come back after two years and was something to stare at in his navy suit, but in a week's time they would be used to him again and put him out of their minds. However, Franklin did not intend to stay around as long as that.

The way Trace had come to have his office at the jail was on account of being arrested for drunkenness all the time. Copper Basin County is dry, but nearby counties are not. Watershed is well served by bootleggers of every stripe: Mister Stiles is obliged to arrest you if you are found drinking, or even with a bottle of whiskey in your possession. (For years Trace got his bootleg liquor from the garbage man, who would empty the garbage can onto his truck, then slip a pint bottle into the empty can before he put the lid back on.) So it was that Trace ended up in a jail cell, time and time again, the morning after. They have to keep a drunk a full twenty-four hours after arrest, even if his name is Tolliver. This naturally played hell with people's dental appointments: Trace had a good many patients who thought he was the best dentist in East Tennessee—rough, but skillful—though he had only studied dentistry in the army, and his entire practice heretofore had been GIs. People in Watershed, and as far away as Pierpont, would a lot rather go to Trace with a hangover than some no-account in Knoxville, dead sober.

Mrs. Stiles, the jailer's wife, swore by him. Trace had done extensive root-canal work on her, and she claimed she could chew like a beaver when he finished with her. It was Mrs. Stiles who thought up letting Trace operate out of a jail cell (though a privileged one, with no bars and his own sink), for the name Tolliver still meant something in Tennessee—even if one of the brothers was a drunk, and the other one peculiar. The motion came up before the Lions Club and they voted on it, and approved. At first it sounded comical to say, "I am on my way to the jail to get my teeth fixed," but after a while it was no more thought of than if Trace still kept his office downtown over the barbershop.

Franklin's spine stiffened when he remembered how he had to inch by those jail cells, flattened against the far wall, to keep out of reach of drunken country boys, mean ones, locked up. If Mrs. Stiles was around, it was all right: she weighed three hundred pounds and carried a blackjack in her apron pocket—but more often than not, she was in her kitchen making dinner for the prisoners.

Franklin had to run down to the jail whenever there was a telephone message for Trace. The Lions Club thought it would be stretching things to let Trace have a telephone listing at the jail, so all his calls came through the home phone at the Tolliver place. Franklin ran back and forth relaying messages. When he came to the jail he had to try and slide by the cells without somebody catching him by the sleeve or the back of his britches.

"You go get me a Co-Cola, you hear?"

If they caught him they could squeeze him up against the bars and hurt him.

"Was you looking cross-eyed at me, penned up in here?"

"If you don't run and get me a pack of cigarettes right quick I'll cut your ears off when I get out of here!"

Just good old boys, everybody said, but wild—though to Franklin they were devils, pure and simple. He had dreams about what they would do to him if they caught him.

Then Franklin's big trouble came along when he was fifteen, and went over to the jail one time to take Trace's mail to him. Without thinking to knock, he walked straight into the little office-cell. There was Billie Jean Ellis sitting in the dentist chair, rolling her silk stockings down. She had already peeled off her blouse and brassiere, like a banana peeled halfway down—her smooth bare skin just as white as the inside of a banana, too. Trace was leaning over Billie Jean, but nowhere near her teeth. He had taken his white dentist jacket off and was pulling his suspenders down—but as soon as he caught sight of Franklin, he pulled them back up. Everybody froze dead still for a second. Billie Jean Ellis made no move to cover herself with the blouse lying in her lap, her big wide mouth open in a silly smile. But Trace gave Franklin a hard look he'd not likely forget. Franklin dropped letters all over the floor, backing out of there.

Here was the very same path Franklin followed Laudermilk down, cemeteries on two sides. The path, when you got past the cemetery, used to be a popular lovers' lane with the young people: if there was a moon it was easier to see from Summit Path than anyplace else, and the woods on that side of Watershed had not yet been touched by the copper fumes—but that was before everybody took to courting in automobiles.

The biggest stone in the "new" cemetery was the Tolliver monument, and beside it the two plots: *Martin B.* and *Clara M.* Clara M. was old Mrs. Tolliver, who half-way brought Franklin up, before she died. She thought up a name for him, herself, and taught him to read and write—for the nearest Colored school was over twenty miles away, and nobody to take him there in an automobile. When Mrs. Tolliver died, Lionel took up Franklin's lessons where she left off. People who knew the family said the Tolliver nigger would probably turn out to be the best educated darky in Tennessee, for the Tollivers were all smart people. Lionel went one step farther; he taught Franklin to read music, to boot.

One time Mrs. Tolliver said to him, "The name Franklin means 'free man'—please think upon that when you feel oppressed, that it may prove your heart's balm." Franklin had thought of it several times since, but it had never proved his heart's balm in the least.

Mrs. Tolliver had always cared more for books than people. She would read out in her hammock on the veranda till the light got too poor to see by or it got too cool to sit out. Then she would take up her cane (she had heart trouble and dizzy spells) and come in, and Franklin would lay a fire for her and take her bottle down from the kitchen cabinet. She always had a toddy of Southern Comfort, with a sugar cube in it, before supper. She was kindly, but not close. She was not even close with her own two boys. When she died, Lionel took all her books to a back room at the courthouse, where they made a library out of them, known as the Clara M. Tolliver Memorial Library to this day.

There were two plots left beside the Tolliver stone, one each for Lionel and Trace.

On the other side of the path, in the "old" cemetery, was that same mausoleum marked MOWBERRY—cracked worse than ever, about to cave in and all grown over with kudzu—where Laudermilk was said to sleep. He could have died and been in there still, for all Franklin knew. Franklin never saw him again after the day he followed him home.

That time, the minute Laudermilk got to the cemetery gate, he spun around on his little platform and fixed his eye on Franklin.

"Where you going, boy?"

"Nowheres."

"You following me?"

Franklin did not answer.

Laudermilk took the harmonica out of his shirt pocket, the same place where Franklin carried his, now. There was a crafty smile on the beggar's face.

"You wished you could play one, don't you?"

"I just like to hear it played."

"You wished you could play one, too."

"Yes sir," said Franklin.

This made Laudermilk smile all the more.

"Well, you never in your life will get to. A nigger's got too thick a lip to play one."

The rainfall in Copper Basin County is said to drain off and flow either to the east or to the southwest, depending on which side of Watershed gets the rain. A geologist who did a survey claimed the actual point of divide ran right through the Tolliver house, in Summit. Rain falling on one side of their roof will run off heading for the Atlantic Ocean. On the other side it will end up in the Gulf of Mexico. Whatever the truth of this was—geological survey or not—the Tolliver place was a house divided.

Mrs. Tolliver had her stroke in 1954, and was found by Franklin in her hammock, dead. She left the house and property and some stock in Consolidated Copper to the two boys, grown men by then. Franklin never knew what

his own momma died of, or when. She had worked for
the Tolliver family all her life, he knew that much. As
for his daddy, there was no telling. Whether the man
had died or just "went off" one time, Franklin would
never know.

Having the Tolliver brothers to answer to was like having two daddies, stern or kindly whichever way the wind
blew—but no kin: each one pulling on you from a different direction. They could be straw bosses both, and keep
Franklin hopping. But they were thoughtful at times, too:
Lionel took pains over Franklin's studies and Trace paid
to have Franklin's tonsils taken out at a Colored clinic in
Chattanooga. They had ambitions for him. Trace wanted
Franklin to turn out a soldier, but Lionel was determined
he would go to Tuskegee Institute come hell or high water. Both brothers had sentimental natures, all told, and
must have loved him, at least in the way a white will love
something that is his, that he has always had, and is black.

When Franklin turned twelve Lionel saw fit to show
him where his momma was buried, and took him to the
very spot. It was not a mound, but a little sunken place in
the lawn at the far end of the Tolliver property—for she
could not be buried in the white cemetery, and there was
no other.

Franklin now came onto the Tolliver place by the
back way, though the boxwood hedge where one boxwood
was missing, right there where his momma was buried.
He stepped quickly across her grave. He had never paid
any particular homage to that place, and he did not now.
After he found out his momma was buried there he
dreaded mowing that corner of the lawn. He just plain did
not like the feeling of the lawnmower running over the
sunken place in the sod.

One reason Franklin came through the back was in

case Billie Jean Ellis might be on the premises. That way, if he had to see her he would see her before she saw him.

He came in behind the house, past the little outhouse that nobody had ever got around to pulling down, and Franklin always used. He was never forbidden the toilet facilities of the main house—plumbing had been put in in 1935—and Franklin had showered himself in the same claw-footed tub Trace and Lionel used, but he had never used the toilet inside. For a black boy who must be mindful not to shout or cry or sing or laugh in front of anybody, a private place, no matter how it smelled, was not easily surrendered.

The main house was a twelve-room two-story pine structure with a steep, shingled roof and no special embellishment except for four square-shaped wooden pillars around the front gallery. As Franklin came around by the side of the house he was relieved to see no car parked out front, which meant Billie Jean Ellis was nowhere in sight—for she did not go ten feet without her car. Through the vines that grew up on that side of the gallery Franklin could make out the two brothers sitting there, each on his own side of the porch. Neither one noticed Franklin's approach. Lionel was lying in his momma's hammock, with a newspaper; Trace sat tilted back in a rocking chair, with a drink in his hand.

They both went on living in that same house: two brothers, as different as night and day. Trace had a belly already, but Lionel at forty-four was as slender as he had been at sixteen. Lionel still had a thick head of hair, though it was naturally going gray; while Trace was getting bald fast, and trimmed what little hair he had left in short-clipped GI fashion.

The Tolliver brothers did not get along. Folks said they did not get along when younger, and that is probably where it started. But the house had been left to them both, and they both decided to live there—though each on his own side of it. Being bachelors, they did not employ the kitchen except to have Franklin make them a sandwich, separately. Trace generally took his meals with Mrs. Stiles, who fed well for a jailer's wife, and Lionel had his meals sent in, or sent Franklin for them, from Hunnicut's Café.

"My lord, lookit who's come!" said Trace, who saw him first. He was speaking to Franklin, not to his brother. The brothers did not speak to one another if they could help it.

"Come up, come up," said Lionel, beckoning to Franklin from the hammock. He snapped his reading glasses off to be certain he was seeing right.

Franklin was suddenly short of breath, for no reason he could think of. He climbed the porch steps as if walking on eggs. He did not take his sailor hat off: he felt better with it on, just as he had when getting off the bus downtown.

"I'm pleased to see you again, Mister Lionel and Mister Trace."

Trace put his feet down on the floor, hard; his face was redder than usual. Lionel tried to smile, but looked uncertain about it. The two brothers were plainly glad to see the black sailor appear before their eyes, though they looked upon him with confusion. It was as if an unexpected wind was blowing across the gallery setting everything astir; or a high piercing note was played on a musical instrument, and stuck there.

"Grown up," said Trace foolishly. "A grown-up man."

"And in the service. Is this a leave you're on, or what?"

"You are a sight for sore eyes."

Franklin's voice came near to failing him as he said, "I just came by to say hello."

"How much leave you got?" asked Trace.

"Nine days, before my ship sails."

"Stay here, stay here," said Lionel. Trace nodded his head yes, in agreement with his brother for once.

"Thank you kindly, but I just came by to say hello. And tell what happened. With me and Miss Ellis. And why I left and what became of Mister Trace's pistol he gave me."

Billie Jean Ellis swore up and down she was going to marry Lionel Tolliver or know the reason why. That was before Trace got out of the army and came home to stay. Billie Jean was in her twenties, and had not got a husband yet. She never would, folks used to say, if she kept on the way she was going. When she turned twenty-one she bought herself a little secondhand red Chevrolet she ran around the country in. She had been known to check into hotels in Chattanooga by herself, but Billie Jean was not the type to stay in a hotel room alone. She came within an inch of being put out of the Baptist church, but what saved her was being piano player for the choir. They say a wide mouth on a woman is a sure sign, and that saying seemed to fit Billie Jean Ellis to a T. She was the talk of the town.

She went with all kinds of men, but never the marrying kind. Where she got the idea to marry Lionel Tolliver nobody could say. He was twice her age, and the tale went around about him that he had once lived with some fellow in Cincinnati, the same as man and wife. Another tale was that Lionel dressed up in his dead momma's clothes, and went to bed in her nightdress. Lionel may have been peculiar, but he was not that peculiar. Franklin had lived too long with the Tolliver brothers to believe every tale that went around about them.

The truth was that Lionel went to Cincinnati to study music at the conservatory up there. He studied piano, and later he played piano accompaniments for concert singers all over the country. But he had a rheumatic heart, and had to quit his career at age thirty-eight. He still played piano two or three hours every day, rain or shine. Lionel was who taught Billie Jean Ellis to play.

"He reminds me of that piano player on television with candles," said Billie Jean, referring to Lionel. "Gray hair on a man is romantic, and I want a husband that's been around."

Then Trace came home, for good.

Trace was more the rough-and-ready type. He did go to Meharry Medical in Nashville for a spell, wanted to be a doctor to start, but changed his mind and settled for dentist when he saw how long an MD took. Then he joined the army in time for the tail end of World War II, but never saw action, and waited around for Korea, but never saw action there either. When his twenty years were up he took his discharge and came out with a good pension. He would never have to work another day of his life, if it suited him not to—but he was restless in Watershed. He went back to his dental practice, only with civilians now instead of soldiers.

"You know something?" said Trace to Franklin. "I always said you would turn up again one of these days."

"Tell Trace he never said any such thing," said Lionel.

The brothers sometimes talked in a childish way, talking through Franklin when they did not agree.

"Whatever made you go and join an outfit like the navy?" asked Trace, who did not bother to hide his disappointment that Franklin was not in an army uniform.

"I just did," said Franklin.

Lionel made no comment one way or the other. His

idea had always been to make a musician out of Franklin, and put him through Fisk or Tuskegee.

"Hell's bells, take a seat," said Trace, and Lionel said, "Yes, sit down, sit down." Lionel was not old, but he had an old man's way of saying things twice.

There was another rocking chair on the veranda, but Franklin felt easier standing up.

Lionel was the one who gave Franklin that harmonica, on his fourteenth birthday.

"It is a Hohner I bought in Cincinnati," said Lionel, "and not just some two-octave toy."

Trace was there when Lionel gave it to him, and snorted in belittlement.

At Christmas, to go Lionel one better, Trace presented Franklin with a .45 pistol he had brought back from the army.

"Now there's a little item that a man can get on in the world with," said Trace.

At first Franklin was too frightened of the thing to pick it up. This was as close as he had ever been to a weapon of any kind. He finally murmured his thanks, then took the pistol in both hands, pointed to the floor, and carried it off, trying to think where to hide it.

There was a fierce dispute between Trace and Lionel over that pistol.

"Are you out of your mind or drunk or what?" Franklin heard Lionel say. "To give a fourteen-year-old colored boy a firearm in this county?"

"That's the goddamn point. Give him confidence, that's what I gave him. Listen, when the going gets rough, he'll go a lot further in this world with a pistol than a mouth organ."

"You are a drunken idiot for sure."

"And you are a piano-thumping ninny. When he gets

older I'm going to get him some cartridges and show him how to shoot the thing."

"Are you out of your mind?"

"Whatever did you do with that pistol then?" Trace was asking. Lionel did not have to ask after the harmonica: it was sticking up in plain sight, out of Franklin's jumper pocket.

"I sold it."

Trace did not say anything for a minute. He reached down into the umbrella stand on the veranda where he kept his bottle, and brought the bottle out. He poured himself another drink, and was about to put the bottle back when he thought to offer a drink to Franklin.

"No, thank you, sir."

"Sold it," Trace repeated to himself. "Live and learn," he said, but he was smiling. Trace took a drink, with the smile still on his face, a trick of his. "Well, you are straightforward about it."

"No, sir, I was not. I sold it to Miss Ellis. She gave me twenty-five dollars for it and asked me where it was so she could go and get it, only I told her the wrong place."

"Billie Jean?" said Lionel.

"Billie Jean Ellis?" repeated Trace. The brothers looked across the porch at one another, something they seldom did if they could help it.

Franklin saw it was high time to tell the whole story.

Billie Jean Ellis started coming around the Tolliver place more and more. Franklin could not stand the sight of her. She claimed she was studying counterpoint and harmony with Lionel, but that was not all she was studying. Also, she was having her teeth fixed by Trace. So between the house and the jail—and sometimes at church, when Franklin worked there and Billie Jean was at choir practice—he was forever crossing her path. He reckoned she was what passed for pretty, with whites. She had an upturned little nose, just barely sprinkled with freckles, that people called cute. She wore sweaters and high heels like a movie star, but there were always dark patches under her eyes as if they had been blacked by somebody, or as if she didn't sleep nights. She most always wore a bandanna on her head, for her dishwater hair was nothing to brag about.

She acted like the new Mrs. Tolliver already, and sent Franklin on fool errands and ordered him around as if he was hers to tell what to do. Half the time she sent him to fetch something she could just as soon get herself, or made up things for him to do just to see him jump.

Franklin had never prayed before and was uncertain how to go about it, but he prayed against Billie Jean Ellis the same as he would have prayed to keep the devil at a distance. He did not believe Lionel would take it in his head to marry such trash, or Trace either, but Billie Jean was devious and determined. You could not bank on anything, for white people were liable to fall for her kind of foolishness. All he could do was try and dodge her, or do what she said when she was around. Meanwhile he prayed she would go off to Chattanooga someday and never come back. But his prayer was not answered, and it seemed like—even in his sleep—he could hear her saying, "Hey, Franklin, come over here."

"Hey, Franklin, come over here." It was Billie Jean Ellis in her red Chevrolet, parked out front of the house.

It was warm for October, and Franklin was barefoot, raking leaves.

"Come over here, I said."

This was right after he had seen her in Trace's office at the jail with her clothes half off. He had a mortal fear of her now, and did not know how to look her in the face. But he put his rake down, and walked slowly down the flagstone path to where she was sitting in the car.

"Get in the car," said Billie Jean.

"I got to rake up these leaves, Miss Ellis."

"Get in. Trace wants you to go to Pierpont with me and help me load up some dental stuff he ordered."

"I better first tell Mister Lionel."

"You get in this car. I just told you what Trace said, and I haven't got all day."

Franklin did not try to hide how miserable he was as he started to get in the back seat.

"Not back there, up front. Where I can talk to you."

"I better not sit in the front, ma'am."

"You better do what I tell you."

Franklin's first thought was to turn tail and run to Lionel, but she had the car door open already, and Franklin did not know how to stop himself from doing what a white person told him to.

He got in, with his stomach churning. She stepped on the gas and the car started so fast the door slammed shut of itself, almost catching Franklin's fingers in it.

They drove through the heart of Watershed like that, Billie Jean Ellis smiling to beat the band and Franklin sitting up front with her. She even turned the radio on, which somehow made it worse.

Franklin squeezed over against the door to be away from her, pressed against the window looking dead ahead, with a frown. He hoped people would think the back seat was loaded, and that was the reason he was up front. A lot of folks saw them in spite of Billie Jean's fast driving —or because of it. The barber stopped cutting somebody's hair to look, and some ladies were looking out the drugstore window. One old man in the center of a bunch of tobacco chewers on the post office steps pointed his cane at the car.

Pierpont, where they were headed, was the county seat and home of the Consolidated Mines, Inc. You used to come across signs in Pierpont saying, "Nigger Don't Let the Sun Set on Your Head in Copper Basin County," to scare blacks off, and keep them from trying for jobs at the mines.

In no time they were through Watershed and out traveling the dead region around Low Point, where nothing was ever known to grow. Hillsides all around were cut across by ugly gullies where the rain had washed all the topsoil away. Not a tree or a blade of grass or a speck of greenery anywhere in sight: fumes from the copper company ate away all the plant life except for a little stretch of experimental vine Consolidated was planting along the highway to keep the roadbed from being washed out altogether.

When they got to the copper works it was worse. Streamers of black and yellow smoke flowed together into one big blistering cloud hanging over the land like a judgment. One main pipe burned a constant hellish smoky flame against the sky; it looked like it would be burning there till doomsday. The smell was so bad you had to roll your windows up. Rusted L&N gondolas were pulled up beside the plant on dead-end railroad tracks, a siding between the slag heaps, where metal chutes could swing out and over the gondolas and load them. But the gondolas stood empty. The only thing pouring out of the plant right then was a mudbank of sludge moving steadily forward, piling up a blue-gray spill on two sides of the tracks. The liquid part of it was some kind of festering sulphur-colored slime that oozed into a ditch beside the road they were driving on. It was like some unholy sore had broken open in the earth and was spilling out a whole river of pus from being so poisoned inside.

The radio in the red Chevrolet was going full blast, and Franklin wanted to cover his ears and squeeze his eyes shut. The sight of this place with a crazy jangle of music coming out of the radio made him feel as scared and low-down as he had ever felt in his life.

The only other soul they saw the whole time was a redheaded hillbilly, stepped out of his jalopy where a rattlesnake had got run over. He looked up from the rattler when Billie Jean's red Chevrolet came by. The look on his face when he stared in at Franklin was as horrible as what was left of the snake.

It dawned on Franklin that Billie Jean Ellis had just made up that errand to Pierpont, Trace had said no such thing. The way she must have dreamed it up was to put Franklin in this fix, on purpose. (He wondered if she was drunk. He had one time seen her drink right out of the bottle, like a man.) No, she was studying some outright meanness—waltzing Franklin through town and now all over the countryside, where people would see him sitting up front with her. There was nothing you would put past her. She was driving Franklin into the worst trouble a black boy could have.

"What do you do with yourself nights, Franklin? I don't see any black gal around Watershed for you to sneak off and be with."

Franklin mumbled something.

"Cat got your tongue?"

"No, ma'am."

She had a foolish giggle for being twenty-some years of age. Franklin could mimic that giggle on his harmonica to sound just like her. (He touched the harmonica in his pocket for luck, seeing as how prayer had failed him.)

Billie Jean then switched radio stations because a gospel program was coming on.

"What'd you think when you saw me that time in my birthday suit?"

"Nothing."

"I bet. I bet you didn't think nothing. I bet you thought plenty."

Franklin tried to scrunch down lower in his seat.

"Did you ever see a shape like mine on somebody before? Did you dream about me, after you saw me like that? Say."

Franklin kept still.

She kept switching radio stations, but none of the songs that came on suited her. Her mood changed like greased lightning.

"Listen here—you going to tell anybody what you saw?"

"No, ma'am."

"I wouldn't care if you did—everybody knows me. Or think they know. I don't give a hoot in hell what they think, except Lionel. I don't want Lionel to know."

"I wouldn't tell him. I swear."

She narrowed her eyes, thinking something over; the dark patches turned darker when she did that. She took out a cigarette and put it in her mouth, driving one-handed. Then she showed Franklin where the cigarette lighter was, and had him light her cigarette for her.

"I fell in love with Lionel Tolliver when I was little, and never got over it," she said, and smoked.

The radio played "You Alway's Said Let's Just Be Friends," so she switched it off.

"Anyway, I got me an idea I want to talk to you about."

Before she could say what her idea was, they came to a

little fairgrounds, with a carnival. It was a strange sight to come across, driving barren territory halfway to nowhere. There was a parking lot with carnival trucks lined up, and a row of cars. All that gaudy out in the midst of this desolation: tents and banners whipped by the wind; neon lights flickering in broad daylight. The ferris wheel was spinning around, with nobody on it. You could hear pinball-machine buzzers all the way out to the road, and country music coming out of loudspeakers.

Billie Jean pulled into the parking lot, still smoking her cigarette.

"You said we were going to Pierpont," said Franklin.

"We're going to Pierpont when I get good and ready."

It was late. A freakish red sun hung low in the smoke haze from the copper works: nothing seemed to cast an actual shadow, not even the ferris wheel. It made you think the carnival and everybody in it would disappear at sundown—but the sun wasn't down yet.

"Come on. Get out of there."

Franklin made no move to leave the car.

Billie Jean smiled her wide smile, her eyes bright and hateful: "I will just have to call on one of these old boys over here to find out what's ailing you."

When he finally got out, his legs felt too weak to walk on. There were mine workers and country people walking the dusty aisles between tents: pinch-lipped wives in their Sunday clothes and frail grandmas in poke bonnets. The men were there, too, wearing overalls or chino pants, their shirt sleeves rolled up. The ladies looked coolly at Billie Jean's high heels and cigarette—the menfolk looked her over, a different way, then switched their gaze to Franklin.

Billie Jean spotted a shooting gallery next to the merry-go-round, and said, "Hey, Franklin, come over here."

Franklin was afraid to stay too far from her and afraid

to stay too close. Everybody on the place was white, of course. Billie Jean took hold of his sleeve and pulled him over to the shooting gallery. The shooting gallery man had an arrow through his head—it was a trick, to attract attention—and tried to talk Billie Jean into shooting at balloons. You could win a French doll or a glass ashtray or a 3-D Plexiglas picture of Christ in the Garden of Gethsemane.

"Not me, sport," said Billie Jean. "Let this boy take a try." She meant Franklin. "He owns his own gun back home, and is a first-class shot."

Franklin's mouth fell open, and stayed that way. Where did she ever find that out? How did she know about the pistol Trace gave him? Trace must have told her himself, bragging—it was just like him.

"I don't know," said the shooting gallery man. He talked out of the side of his mouth and you could tell he was not from Tennessee. He was puzzled about handing over a rifle to a colored boy, even a shooting gallery rifle. "Why don't you try, yourself. Only thirty-nine cents, five shots."

But Billie Jean had picked up one of the rifles and held it out to Franklin, as far as the chain would go.

The shooting gallery began to draw a restless crowd. When Billie Jean said, "Show these folks what a good shot you are," a bunch of white-headed kids heard her, and slid down from their wooden ponies and spilled off the merry-go-round before it could even come to a stop. They gathered around, somber, watching to see if a black boy was really going to shoot a rifle.

A hillbilly lament was coming out of the merry-go-round loudspeaker, but all of a sudden it faded out and the merry-go-round came to a dead stop. Out of the corner of his eye Franklin saw a man step down off the merry-go-round platform: he was wearing a Gene Autry cow-boy shirt and was the living image of Laudermilk, only he had legs. His arms were big like Laudermilk's, and he came up and stood nearby with his big arms crossed across his chest, waiting.

The shooting gallery man did not want any trouble, and kept saying, "I don't know, miss," to Billie Jean. The arrow through his head would swing one way and then another as he watched how the crowd was building up. "Tell you what," he said, with a worried smile, "how about you yourself taking a few potshots, on the house, no charge."

Then the merry-go-round man spit tobacco between his feet, and spoke up.

"That nigger work for you, little lady?"

"What's it to you?" Billie Jean snapped back. She would sass the devil himself, if she met up with him.

The merry-go-round man did not even uncross his arms. He just switched his cud from one side of his mouth to the other, and said: "That boy ain't going to shoot no rifles around here. Now, I am giving you five minutes to get your nigger out of this here carnival before we take and string him up from a telephone pole."

Franklin's legs just about buckled on him. The crowd murmured in an ugly way, backing the merry-go-round man up. Sweat and tears poured down Franklin's face, and in a minute he would have keeled over.

But then Billie Jean had sense enough to know she had gone too far. She stamped her cigarette out under a spike heel, mad, and stalked off through a place in the crowd. Franklin stumbled after her. Nobody laid a hand on him, or tried to, and he somehow got to the car safe and sound.

He thought the automobile would never get started, but it did, while he was holding onto his harmonica, next to his heart. The carnival music started up the same time as the motor.

* * *

"Just the kind of dangerous stunt that damn fool would pull," said Lionel, aroused, sitting up straight as a poker. His newspaper had come apart all over the hammock.

Trace just sat looking sheepish and uneasy.

"She drove me directly to Pierpont after that," said Franklin. "On the way over she said, 'Well, you see the fix you are in. I reckon you better hightail it out of this county, if you know what is good for you.' I think I started to cry. She had got me so mixed up I didn't know where I was at. But I sure enough knew I had to go off. She said, 'I tell you what, I'll buy that pistol off of you.' She was smiling when she said it. 'I never got no place playing piano,' she said. 'Maybe a pistol is what I need.' Then she laughed and said, 'I'll give you twenty-five dollars for it, which will buy you a bus ticket to a place where there's more niggers than you can shake a stick at, where you'll feel right at home.' As soon as we got to Pierpont she drove me straight to the bus station. She asked me where the pistol was hid, and I said upstairs under my straw tick where I slept. Then she counted out twenty-five dollars in fives in my hand, and bought me a bus ticket to Washington, D.C."

Trace went on looking sheepish, if a little stunned, but Lionel was as mad as if it had happened yesterday: "You mean she sent you off to Washington without any shoes on your feet?" What he could not get over was that Franklin went on the bus barefoot.

"A lady at Traveler's Aid in Washington got me a pair when I got there, and a room at the YMCA."

"You sure you don't want a drink?" asked Trace, who was having another himself. He had his bottle all the way out of the umbrella stand, and kept it wedged between his knees, handy.

"No, sir, thank you kindly."

"He thinks everything in life is smoothed over with a drink of whiskey. Him and his whiskey and guns."

Trace merely sipped his whiskey, looking out through the vines into nowhere.

"You hear me?" Lionel directed himself to his brother. "You like to got this boy killed."

"Keep it up, keep it up," said Trace, tilted back. "No use crying over spilt milk."

Lionel glared at him, then lapsed into silence. Trace began rocking slowly in the rocking chair while Lionel put his newspaper back together.

"For unadulterated evil, that woman takes the cake."

"She was a wild one, all right," said Trace.

There was another silence while Franklin wondered what had become of her.

Then Trace spoke up and said, "Well, anyway, she took off"—without Franklin's having to ask.

"I hope she's in hell," said Lionel.

"Wherever she is, she's making hell for somebody. She took up with a married man with a motorcycle, a grease monkey from Low Point—and the last anybody heard, the two of them run off on his Honda with every penny the man could lay his hands on."

"The wife is now on welfare," said Lionel, "and two children."

"She surely was a wild one," said Trace, as if the world was full of wild women, and what you had to do was watch your step. "I wonder if she has shot her grease monkey yet, with that pistol you sold her."

"No, sir, not with that pistol. I told her it was under my straw tick, but it never was."

They waited for Franklin to say where he kept it.

"You know, Mister Trace, I was scared of that thing from the start. I never wanted to touch it. A long time ago, not long after you gave it to me, I threw that pistol down the hole out in the privy where I always went. Nobody shoot anybody with that pistol."

Lionel was the first to smile, a look of pure satisfaction on his face. Then Trace began to chuckle low to himself —Franklin's tale beginning to sink in, thinking how things turn out—but he soon got to laughing so hard Franklin feared he would tip over in his rocking chair. His face went crimson from laughing and he spilled whiskey all over his pants. Pretty soon he worked up a coughing spell. Lionel looked disgusted with him, but Franklin went over and slapped him on the back the way he used to do, to get him his breath back before he strangled. He took the bottle from between Trace's legs and put it back in the umbrella stand where it wouldn't get broken.

There was no further talk of Franklin staying his leave time at the Tolliver place. The brothers knew, as well as Franklin, the time was up and the long watch was over. Whatever else Billie Jean Ellis had brought about in these parts, she had managed to set Franklin apart from Watershed forever. He had only come back, as he said, to say hello.

Trace tried to get up out of his rocking chair when he shook Franklin's hand good-by, but he was too drunk or too weak to. There was pain in Lionel's eyes when he let go of Franklin's hand, but he was dignified about it. That was how Franklin left them, each on his own side of the veranda; and as he walked down the flagstone walk he could not help but notice how poorly the lawn was kept.

At the bus station Franklin sat on a divan made out of a car seat and practiced how to make a harmonica sound like a white man's laugh.

Littlejohn is tapping the harmonica against his hip, to clear the instrument of spit. The song he has finished is not what was expected. There is a little spell of quiet, a silence made all the deeper with the music missing.

"What the hell song was that?" asks Bailey.

"That's some country music of mine."

"Say what you like," says the helmsman, "but Little-john can sure in hell play a mouth organ."

"Is that what's called semiclassical?" asks the relief helmsman, and the helmsman says, "No, semiclassical is like 'White Christmas.' What Littlejohn played is more on the order of what they call folk songs."

"How do the words go?" asks Bailey.

"That song is a song I wrote myself. I never wrote the words to it."

"Interesting," says Mister Walker. "Now, I always thought you people specialized in the blues." Mister Walker has never known exactly what the blues are.

"Not always," says Littlejohn, "sir."

It is 0325 hours, and the midwatch is almost up. It is high time for Littlejohn to go around the ship waking up the four-to-eight relief. He tucks the harmonica into the jumper pocket of his whites, and is about to go below when the helmsman says, "What the hell, take the wheel for a little while. Get some steering practice. I'll wake the relief for you."

"Good idea," says Bailey, who is Littlejohn's division PO and has for some time been thinking of letting Little-john stand a wheel watch.

"Permission granted," says Mister Walker, whose permission has not been requested.

Bailey is obliged to complete the ship's log before the watch is over, so it falls to the relief helmsman—still wearing Littlejohn's headset—to stand at Littlejohn's shoulder and instruct him as to the function of the steering gear. Mister Walker tells Littlejohn what course they are on, then walks out onto the flying bridge to scan the

34

horizon with his binoculars in case the lookout may have missed a last-minute light. Littlejohn's hand trembles on the polished spoke of the ship's great wheel, and the relief helmsman says, "Don't worry, everybody is nervous at first."

Littlejohn's dark face, illuminated from below by the shaded light from the gyrocompass, is set in concentration as he takes in the words of the relief helmsman. At the same time he is trying to forget several ghostly faces that continue to bedevil him, and shake himself from the echo of music still lingering in the wheelhouse. The relief helmsman puts one hand on the wheel with Littlejohn's: one full swing to the right, then a half-turn back to correct the swing. Littlejohn can feel the ship's vibration through the soles of his feet as the *Halstead* responds to the steering maneuver.

In a little while the relief helmsman takes his hand from the wheel and stands away. The black sailor is alone, steering the USS *Halstead* through the deep waters of a southern sea.

The Man Who
Wrote Letters to Presidents

TO CELEBRATE the beginning of his new mustache, Paul Greer stopped off at the Hasta la Vista after work. At forty-three he was growing bald in the front and thought a mustache would compensate for the loss, but as soon as he saw his image in the mirror behind the bar he realized the shadow under his nose had simply changed his face from a cipher to a cipher with a line in the center. Forty-three years of nothing showed in Paul Greer's face, and the growth on his upper lip was no help.

There was not another customer in the place, and the air conditioning touched him with a tomblike chill. He should have beaten a retreat on that first impulse of disappointment, but Jesús, the bartender, had already greeted him and whipped into action. A gin-and-tonic appeared on the bar in front of Paul Greer's favorite stool. Jesús was a newcomer to the U.S., but he was already a bartender of the old school. And Paul Greer, being Paul Greer, could never resist an operation already under way.

He decided to have just this one, then walk over to Indian Creek Drive and check the paint job on his car for scratches, to use up a little more of the dead part of the evening—and was drinking to that thought when an old man's voice asked out of the darkness, "What's your Social Security number, partner?"

"What?" But before Paul Greer could stop himself he was reciting: "402-30-9672."

"Shake, partner. You're the first one I ever met that could reel off their numbers as good as me." The old man moved from stool to stool until he was sitting next to Paul Greer. He thought he might have seen this old man in the hotel kitchen earlier, on the afternoon shift, running racks of dessert plates into the dishwashing machine. Paul Greer was a salad chef at the Crown Jewel on Collins Avenue.

"Meet 105-78-3110. Born loser. I lost my very first Social Security card I wasn't ten minutes out of their office. Hole in my pants you could run your fist through. They cussed me out good, but they had to refund me another one. I memorized all my numbers after that. Say, what's your time-card number?"

"274. Why?"

"I'm 885. New man. Temporary only. They'll give me the old heave-ho the first Cuban deflected from Cuba comes along."

Paul Greer felt the old man's shriveled paw pick up his hand and shake it. He hoped Jesús had not heard the slur about Cubans, but Jesús had walked out of earshot after moving the old man's beer down from the other end of the bar. Now, with the glass of beer next to his gin-and-tonic, Paul Greer felt himself committed to his bar stool, trapped between the old man and the cash register. He drank, but not even the quinine could cancel out the old-man smell of sour beer and dishwater. Why couldn't Kathleen, the new cashier, come in? Or Mildred, the cocktail waitress from the Crown Jewel? No, it was Paul Greer's unfailing misfortune to fall in with another zero like himself, elbow to elbow, at the Hasta la Vista.

"In '29 I was living on ragweed salad and boiled swamp root. You should've seen me. My stomach was swelled up like nobody's business. I wrote President Hoover if he didn't quick send me a Care pack and a bag of tobacco I was done for, to just go ahead and subtract my number from the U.S. Census."

If he said nothing the old man would go away, but he could not keep himself from asking, "Did he answer?"

"Hell, yes, he answered, they have to. Afraid you won't vote for them next time around. He wrote and referred me to welfare, which didn't exist in Florida yet. It was only '29. They answer all right. Their letter paper's got an eagle on it to look official."

As a matter of fact, Paul Greer had been expecting another depression any year now—two depressions were none too many to predict in any loser's lifetime, so he asked—in case he could use the information later on—"What did you do then?"

"Only thing a man *can* do when he's down to rock bottom without a paddle, went and broke a beer bottle on a street curb in Tampa and swallowed two big jagged pieces of it in public. That way you bring your case to the attention of the authorities. Must've been a crowd of fifty seen me do it and not one son-of-a-bitch amongst them stepped forward to volunteer first aid. That's how far apart people have fell. Finally a cop came and put me under arrest—when he has to, a cop'll take action, provided he's in his home precinct and not on his lunch hour. They operated and got the glass out of me, and I ended up in a nice bed with clean sheets and my own radio to listen to. They fed good, too, for a hospital."

Paul Greer's eyes had adjusted now to the meager light, and he stared at the jockey-size figure perched on the bar stool beside him. His stomach felt cold, as if he had swallowed an ice cube from his drink: the old man's face could have been his own—change the color of the eyes, take away Paul Greer's new mustache, and add thirty years of dried scars and mournful wrinkles.

"What's your service number, by the way?"

"280-90-90."

"Mine's 63-49017. They had a different series the First World War. In 1919 I got drunk in a little Belgian town nobody could pronounce, before they blew it up, and the next day went and tried to go over the top with a wine hangover, the worst kind, and got gassed. I later tried to get disability out of it. I wrote President Wilson, but he suffered a stroke signing peace treaties in Paris, and the First Lady, his wife, Mrs. Wilson herself, wrote and referred me back to the army. My pension forms must've went through two-hundred-some-odd secretaries and file clerks and chief assistant flunkies—Washington's probably got reels and reels of microfilms on me—till seven years later the VA wrote and told me no, it was my own negligence. Eye witness from my own company said I went and forgot my gas mask. That's the kind of lovable buddies you had the First War."

Paul Greer had an urge to contribute a war reminiscence of his own, and tell about being a Baker, second class, in the South Pacific, when a Japanese mine exploded fifty yards from his destroyer's bow—but the loss of four oven racks of bread loaves could not compare with the high tragedy of trench warfare; anyway, the old man was still talking.

"Don't think I always just wrote letters to Presidents to get goodies for yours truly. I one time wrote Roosevelt if he didn't get his CCC boys off the Florida Keys they'd get blowed off. A pal of mine was a pure-blood Seminole Indian and he knew a hurricane coming when he smelt one. The government's always the last one to get the word. Every single flamingo in the Everglades was flying north and the goddamn dumb government wouldn't listen to the evidence. Left all them boys, I don't know how many, down at Islamoralda in a fly-by-night CCC camp."

Jesús had put pretzels and potato chips on the bar, and Paul Greer was building a tepee out of pretzel twigs to keep from cracking his knuckles or biting his fingernails.

"What finally happened?"

"Happened? What finally happened was the biggest awful blow in the history of Florida, and all them stranded CCC boys got washed out to sea on a tidal wave."

The force of the old man's indignation had blown Paul Greer's tepee apart.

"But didn't Roosevelt answer?"

"Hell, yes, they always *answer*. They got a answering service and a hundred-and-fifty geniuses to write answers. You can't fool me, all the President does is sign his name. Me and my Indian buddy was sitting out the hurricane in Homestead when I got their telegram, two days late, said, 'All necessary precautions have been taken stop grateful for your concern stop etcetera.' That's the government for you."

Paul Greer drank his drink down to the bare cubes—he did not want to hear any more. The Hasta la Vista was no place to come to listen to depressing stories: there was enough of that on TV. What he would do, he would walk over to Indian Creek Drive and check the air pressure in his tires, but the old man put his worn-out-tennis-shoe hand on Paul Greer's arm, saying, "Don't worry. They put up a real nice memorial monument for them—which is a hell of a lot more'n you and me'll get—and every year the ladies from the Florida Historical Society puts a pot of wax flowers on it, first week in hurricane season."

Paul Greer wanted to pay and slide away from the bar, but Jesús had drifted from behind the cash register to plug in the pinball machine and jukebox. He was unable to summon Jesús—had his vocal cords been affected by drinking the gin-and-tonic too quickly?—for he could not speak. The old man's voice, on the contrary, went on and on.

"Down in Key West one time on the bum I tried to get a job in the U.S. Post Office. They're supposed to give you veteran's preference if you've fought a war to bring peace to mankind, but the First War's too old fashion and long forgot for them. They give my mailman job out to a Young Republican. I was sore as boils and wrote Harry S. Truman about it—I always admired that motto on his desk that said, 'The buck stops here'—and he referred me to Civil Service. Civil Service didn't like my looks on account of I didn't have no necktie on, or on account of my tattoo, this here rattlesnake, or I don't know what, so they put me in their file and winked at each other and forgot about me."

In the watery neon light reflected from the jukebox, Paul Greer could make out the pale blue reptile coiled along the old man's forearm and the legend tattooed above his wrist that read: "Don't Tread on Me!"—a warning the world had apparently ignored.

"Nothing I could do but bring my case to the attention of the local authorities. I swallowed a fishhook in plain view of a church letting out from Sunday service. The entire congregation ringed theirself around me like I was a diversion from the Sunday dumps—a free circus or some-thing—me turning blue and spitting blood all over the church steps, and nobody offered an encouraging word. You read about that waitress up north that got stabbed to death in a parking lot with fifty people watching from their windows, nobody come forth or even call a cop? Well, the hospitality is the same down south. The preacher, he finally showed up to find out what the hullabaloo was all about, and seen me, and said gentle-like, 'Why'd you do it, old-timer?' then stepped back so as not to get blood on his shoeshine. You know what?"

Paul Greer admitted he did not.

"I finally had to stagger into a phone booth and call an ambulance up myself, in my condition. They operated on me again. All told, I've had six probe-surgery operations. My stomach looks like a road map, look."

The old man pulled the T-shirt out of his belt to allow Paul Greer the full panorama of surgical scars twisted across the old man's abdomen. You had to give the old boy credit for survival against all odds. The only visible evidence Paul Greer had to show for being a victim of the system was the nicks in his thumbs from carving radishes into rosettes.

"Let me tell you something, and I mean it. When I go to the VA or Unemployment, or if I go into Social Se-curity or the Red Cross or Salvation Army or anyplace, I want the girl behind the desk to treat me like a human man and give me ordinary decent respectfulness like I deserve. By God, I'm a human man with a name and a face and feelings like everybody else. I'm not looking for some snotty clerk at the counter to call me 'you' or 'next' or a number. I've had Presidents of the United States to call me Mister, and they almost always got my name right, too."

Speaking of names, Paul Greer would like to have told the old man about his father, Henri Grenadier, who lost his restaurant to creditors in Lyons, took steerage passage for the new world, and how his name was reduced to Henry Greer passing through Immigration on Ellis Island—but the old man was too wound up to deal with the petty grievances of a long-dead foreigner.

"And another thing. This goddamn numbers racket gets my goat. By the time you're my age you got so many numbers attached to you, you look like a laundry list. Only way a man can fight back is carry a ticket puncher in his pocket and every time you get hold of an IBM card, punch hell out of the bastard. That's how you throw a monkey wrench in their machinery. Catch me using a zip code? Hell, I don't even put a zip code on the President's letters.

"Listen, it's not all gravy for yours truly, keeping up a correspondence with the Chief Executive. I write to try and get a flyspeck of attention turned onto all the old drifters washed up on U.S. shores, left behind down in the doldrums, like me. Why, I believe I'd rather go in front of a firing squad than go into one more government file—I'm damn near buried in case numbers as it is already."

The only thing Paul Greer could think of to make the establishment bleed a little (the old man's ticket punch was too farfetched) was to cancel his application for a Diner's Club credit card, still pending.

"You won't believe this but I once dove for sponges off Sarasota with the Greeks till I got too old to hold my breath. I went back one season, '55 I think it was, to work the boats with them, but plastic sponges had come in and the natural sponge trade went to the devil. Try selling a genuine real-life sponge to a woman nowadays, she'll throw you right off the porch. Housewives don't know nothing about housekeep that they didn't read in the magazines or see on TV."

The word housewife reminded Paul Greer of his brief marriage during the war, seventeen days all told (the so-called honeymoon crowded into a three-day pass in Albuquerque), that ended with a Dear John letter on a V-mail postal form.

"Anyway, me and this Greek family I was living with, we got down to four dollars with seven mouths to feed, not counting yours truly. We ate spoilt tomatoes till we was sweating tomato juice. Made a whole meal onetime out of boiled potato peels. You can always pick up a coconut out of the gutter for dessert, but who's got the strength starving to death to crack one open? Before they'd have to put their oldest girl out on the street for a whore, I got hold of a post-office pen and wrote Eisenhower a four-page letter. My mistake was I went and forgot it was McCarthy's heydays, and for an answer I got an FBI guy knocking on our door to find out if any of us was Communists. The Greeks threw me out on my ear for getting them investigated—can't hardly blame them, they'll have a black mark in Washington for the rest of their life. The FBI warned me I was a known crank from then on and under strict surveillance and if I didn't watch my step I'd lose my mail privilege and my passport." Tears sprinkled into the old man's beer glass. "After that I sort of lost touch with the White House."

A potato chip had been on the way to Paul Greer's mouth but never got there. He began crushing it to powder in his fist.

"My last job I took a job night watchman of a parking lot in Coral Gables—try living on sixty-five fifty a month Social Security sometime, if you want to live dangerous— but I got sick and tired of being called Whitey and Shorty and Pop and went and let the air out of some snot's tires one night, so they fired me."

The gullies in the old man's face ran wet with tears, and Paul Greer tried to summon up a word of sympathy, but could think of nothing comforting except to offer the old fellow another beer.

"The last letter I ever wrote a President, or ever will write, I wrote to Kennedy—but some son-of-a-bitch down in Dallas killed him before he could answer me."

The old man dropped his hands to his hips and in a sudden fumbling spasm emptied his pockets onto the bar: a dirty khaki handkerchief, some small change (mostly dimes), a mimeographed ID card from the Homestead Employment Agency, a bus driver's ticket punch, and a safety pin.

"I swallowed a whole box of staples one time, but I just vomited them back up again. Last year I went and swallowed a bottle of nail polish, bottle and all, and they had to fish it out, out at the VA Hospital. The doc out there, he kept calling me old-timer, which always gets my goat. 'Old-timer,' he says, 'one of these days you're liable to swallow one dangerous object too many.' Trying to use psychiatry on me. To needle him I said, 'What about a nice big opened-up safety pin?' and he got sore and said, 'You swallow a pin and it's liable to catch in your gullet and work and pierce you right in the heart.' What he meant was he wished I would."

Maybe if he gave the old man ten dollars he would go away, and Paul Greer was reaching for his billfold when the old man picked up the safety pin and said, "See this here pin? It turned up in my clothes bag in the laundry-mat, must've come off some kid's diapers. They put a plastic safety catch on them now so they won't accidental open up and stick your baby."

He opened the plastic catch to show Paul Greer how it

worked. Then he rocked backwards on the stool, opened wide his toothless mouth, and dropped the safety pin into it. He rocked forward again. With a terrible gagging sound, the old man washed the pin down with a swallow of beer.

Paul Greer went numb. He tried to remember whether the pin had been opened or closed when the old man swallowed it. Not since the explosion of the Japanese mine reverberated through the ship's bakery had he known a panic like the panic he felt now. Surely the pin was closed, there was a safety catch on it so you wouldn't stick your baby. When the numbness passed, and he could act on his resolve, Paul Greer fled the bar.

Somehow, with no recollection of the interval, Paul Greer found himself sitting safely behind the wheel of his powder-blue Continental, parked in the luxuriant shade of a coconut palm. He did not try to start the car. His pencil mustache was wet with perspiration, and somewhere between the Hasta la Vista and Indian Creek Drive his legs seemed to have dropped off at the knees. The smell of the sun-baked automobile interior sustained him for now: he would be all right in a little while, he told himself.

He reminded himself of his accomplishments: he was a man who could make a mayonnaise in twelve seconds, provided the vegetable oil was pure and the egg had not been refrigerated. He had been awarded the Good Conduct medal by the U.S. Navy; his car would be absolutely paid for in four more payments. Once—and this was the high point in his career—he had supervised as many as seven hundred lettuce-and-tomato salads for a single Veterans of Foreign Wars luncheon, with Thousand Island dressing, and not one wilted lettuce leaf by the time the salads were served.

He sat cracking his knuckles and chewing on his mustache until he heard the ambulance siren coming across the causeway at Arthur Godfrey Road. It was then he began writing frantic letters in his head, "Dear Mr. President"—but whether to write about the old man's downfall or his own he did not know.

A Soliloquy in Tongues

I

BILLBOARDS ALL SAID JESUS in brackets
with Little Sister, made you think Jesus *and* Little Sister
Saves—Joe was the one that thought up those posters.
Around at camp meetings everybody called him Daddy
Joe, to go with Little Sister. That was a pair of dudes, the
two of them, believe you me. Joe, he was general manager
in charge of the Glory Road (how he wangled us into the
National Southern Revival Association beats me), carried
a mail-order ministry license in his hip pocket (never
even graduated high school), and that slicker could talk
the vest buttons off a district attorney. On top of everything else, Joe did interpretations for Little Sister working
mainly out of the American language, but he talked

tongues to the general public. He talked me out of a hundred and sixty-five dollars once. And into hot water besides. But our last argument I got him good and told off when he called me Satan's mistress.

"What's that got to do with the price of eggs?" says I right back. "Little Sister still happens to be my little girl."

She's his, too, but *I'm* the mother.

They run out on me in Chattanooga, Tennessee. Just folded their tent like an Arab and went off to Knoxville in the night. I got a private detective on them until he got drunk in Copper Hill, and since then I've had to go it alone. I blew into Knoxville two and a half hours after they left town. Then I tracked them across the Georgia state line at Gainesville, but after that they quit running meetings at county seats and went to working one-horse towns too little even to have parking meters. A cab driver in Dahlonega told me they'd set up a healing campaign in a little dumpy town called Clay Ridge, but by the time I found out how to get there they'd healed everybody in sight and took off again. (That must've been when Joe commenced teaching Little Sister how to heal. Joe's smart as the dickens that way—he knows good and well you can't hardly beat healings with anything less than a genuine resurrection.)

To multiply insults with injuries I went broke in Clay Ridge and I've heard tell these hick towns are mean as sin to vagrants, so I was obliged to work waiting tables at a juke joint called the Mountain Rim Café. But I worked some of my spite off writing anonymous letters to the AMA with complete descriptions right down to Joe's black bow-ribbon tie and the taps on Little Sister's shoes (and told how they specialized in cancer cures with laying-on of hands). I never got no answer.

Then a trucker was having Sunday dinner at the Mountain Rim told me he knew of a traveling preacher with a little girl healer down around Marietta. I turned in my apron and took a Trailways on the spot. There was frequent rest stops at Tate and Canton and Ballground, and I had a pint of sugar liquor in my pocketbook that helped me digest my bile in the Lady's Room.

The only remainders of her and Joe left around in Marietta was unpaid hotel and dry-cleaner bills and a week-old poster posted up on a telephone pole. It was a different poster now, and featured a new picture of Little Sister—with a halo all the way around her head—but I recognized her.

I knew they'd skip Atlanta. Atlanta's got ordinances. But I stayed over to stay for a picture show starring Doris Day, my favorite actor.

My big mistake after that was a man I met in Griffin, claimed he owned a lumber mill. Why, he didn't even own his own toothpicks, let alone lumber, and I paid for every can of Budweiser that man drank. He delayed me over a week and when I got to Macon they said the revival campaign went south two Sundays ago and took the town's leading choir soloist, age sixteen (Methodist), along with them. Her momma told me, "She looked like a real debutante, her hair was the color of cornbread, that child could sing like a nighting-gale," and she busted out crying. She thought the white slavers had got her, but I said it was just Joe.

Down around Waycross I figured they'd cross across the Florida line, and they did. A filling station man at the Last Chance filling station just this side of the Okefenokee Swamp said he give them gas and got a rubber check for his trouble.

"Twenty gallon-a-gas and I don't know how many cans of diesel oil and either that brat or this blonde puked all over my comfort station."

He claimed they had a Mack truck and a Chrysler convertible—I don't know where they got the money for a new truck and a Chrysler, all Joe ever drove before was a busted-up Ford station wagon with the wood panels all eat out—and he showed me their last poster which they accidental left behind and he was saving for evidence if they ever came through Waycross again. The newest added attraction on that poster was The Silver-Voice Gospel Quartet featuring Miss Clara Joy Sims, coloratura soprano, and a picture of Clara Joy Sims in a low-neck dress showing off her bosoms with three hillbillies behind her with their mouth open in a yodel. That picture got my goat. But Little Sister, my own little girl, was on top, wearing her same halo and still the star.

By now I was getting smart. I took the first Greyhound out of town and got to Miami two weeks before they did.

II

They advertised as the world's biggest gigantic gospel tent, and it looked it, stretched out over half an acre of Broward County (Joe knew better than to set up on the Dade County side) halfways between Hialeah and the Opa-Locka airport. I had took a real nice room at the Opa-Locka Motor Courts with TV and all air-conditions, just biding my time drinking ice-cold Cokes with vodka chasers and writing anonymous postcards to the Jr. Chamber of Commerce to warn them that the Glory Road was moving down the Tamiami Trail. But the JayCees are located on the Dade County side, so they didn't give a hoot in hell about Joe or anybody else, on the Broward side. Your average businessman, all they're looking out for is number one. I must've wrote fifty cards, and half of them had color flamingos on one side, to catch people's attention. But I never got no answer.

For the rest, I just kept under covers. A private eye couldn't've been more secret than me. I wasn't speaking two words to nobody except my liquor store man in Little River where I bought my vodka, and acted like I wasn't even in town. I'm Pisces the Fish, and the very night the revival opened for business my *Miami Herald* horoscope said: "A time for settling accounts. Move forward. Direct action is indicated for ventures already under way. Take advantage of aggressive forces during this period to improve personal relationships." In other words, take your bull by the horns. Joe's Taurus.

So I was right there standing in line opening night of the revival and like to got squashed in the crowd.

Well, there was Little Sister sitting up big as bounce on a baby throne in the middle of a plank-and-sawhorse stage with a pure gold halo wired to her Shirley Temple curls and a bunch of lily-of-the-valleys in her lap. She was cute as the devil in her white angel robe sitting there scratching her elbow with one hand and holding a King James Bible in the other. Everything, including Little Sister, was lit up like a high-class funeral, with every imaginable light fixture and a real neon sign saying THE LORD WORKS IN MYSTERIOUS WAYS which they must've run out of neon to end with HIS WONDERS TO PERFORM, and a whole rotater-sunset of colored lights fastened to the main tent poles beaming flicker-flack down on the congregation like you see at a fancy dance hall—only here it represents Glory. (I don't know who Joe's electrician was, but whoever he was he was tops.)

It did my heart good to see that Miss Clara Joy Sims must've been took with the virus that was going around Broward County because The Silver-Voice Gospel Quartet had went down to a trio, and all there was left was the hillbillies singing "When the Roll Is Called Up Yonder" barbershop style, which by the time I got to a folding chair that wasn't too tilted from the sawdust to sit down in, they switched to "He's Got the Whole World in His Hands," with their hands out. In about a minute here comes Daddy Joe hisself out from behind a curtain in a brand-new shantung silk suit so shiny it like to put your eyes out, cracking his portable microphone wire out from underfoot like a whipsnake. The microphone mouthpiece was strung around his neck (I wished it was a noose) like a tobacco auctioneer's, to magnify him telling everybody to ring the rafters (there wasn't no rafters, it was only a tent) with Introduction Hymn Number 129. You couldn't get hold of a hymnal for love nor money unless you tipped one of the ushers for one, but everybody knew the words anyway, and Little Sister slid down from her throne still attached to her Bible (but quit scratching) and stood there with the Gospel Trio in a big spotlight to lead the singing. Here was I traveled all them miles to work out my meanness, but I *was* proud as peaches of my little girl. She couldn't've looked cuter if she tried. I don't know where she gets it from—Joe's black-headed, and I'm what they call dishwater—but Little Sister is a natural-born albino blonde.

The singing was real nice, I admit.

But what got me sore was Joe up there big as brass acting humble before the Lord, standing to one side of the Gospel Trio moving his lips like he was singing (Joe can't carry a tune in a basket) with about two hundred dollars' worth of silk suit on his good-for-nothing hide.

They skipped two verses to sing last verse and refrain, and when the Hammond electric organ got done playing a beautiful tricky Amen, Joe went directly into Heart Prayers before anybody got a chance to start coughing. The tent went quiet as a tomb and all you could hear was the Miami mosquito-spray plane humming over Hialeah. Everybody bent their head down but me. Little Sister was

down on her knees with her snow-white angel dress
puffed out around her little hips like a mushroom. Her
Bible was balanced on her lap so it wouldn't touch the
floor and she had her hands pressed real sweet together in
prayer, but from the way she kept rubbing her arm
against her side you could tell her elbow still itched.

Joe blessed everybody that ever lived, including the
sick and weary, arthritis victims (at least twenty people
said "Amen!"), retired firemen, convicts and thiefs, politicians, backsliders and general chronic lost souls, and a
special Heart Dedication to soldiers out on far-flung bat-
tlefields and our boys in navy blue on the various seven
seas that guard our proud shores from foreign Communists and those who would undermine the American way
of life and enslave us. By now there was a lot of people
calling out "Amen!" so Joe finally took the hint and said
"Amen!" hisself. There was a typical unholy racket of
everybody sitting back down in their folding chairs.

Then the organ played "Because" so slow and sweet not
a baby cried anywheres, while Sister climbed back up on
the throne and laid her lilies back down in her lap and
the Gospel Trio walked dignified offstage. That left only
Daddy Joe in the spotlight (his favorite place), so he
bowed his head down as if checking his shoeshine, and
finally even the organ faded out, trembly and sanctified.

Says I to myself, now's your chance, and was all set to
stomp up the aisle and say a few choice words into Joe's
portable microphone, but I timed my timing all wrong.
This was always when Joe did Fellowship Announce-
ments to attract new fellowships (funds, in other words)
into the Kingdom. But Joe all of a sudden reared back
cracking his electric wire at the devil and scared the livers
out of me and everybody else with a: "M-a-a-ano-
mano-manofallibillofalliabbabba! PRAISE God! SWEET
Jesus!"

I couldn't budge. It like to took the curl out of my permanent wave. A deaf-mute on my left tuned down his hearing aid to hear.

Then a: "O-O-Orgiabillabba-amofine! SWEET Jesus A-a-a-men!"

You see, he'd already went into transfiguration and was starting to talk in tongues.

Crack! Somebody's folding chair collapsed, and I saw down my row where a crippled old grandma was down in the sawdust. She wasn't hurt none, though, for she kept yelling: "Sweet HEAL-o-HEAL-o-HEAL-o. THANK you Jesus!" and went crawling forward on all fours with her pocketbook clamped in her armpit.

That old lady (you couldn't help but wonder if Joe put her up to it) set off a firecracker string of miracles, and a man with dropsy led a parade down the center aisle in a power-motor wheelchair. It was a tragical conglomeration of sinners and sick people, drunkards, terminal cancers and for instance a blind old man leading a blind old lady down to the sawhorses—and right behind them two trained nurses toting a backwards child on a canvas contraption that obliged the audience by climbing off his canvas seat and having an epileptic fit down by the Hammond organ.

Why, you could've stocked a whole Jackson Memorial Hospital with that crowd and still've had enough sick leftovers to fill two wings of Miami Sanitarium. I wouldn't't've been any too surprised to see a lineup of lepers come forth to be healed. Rheumatisms and alcoholics was peanuts to this bunch. Whatever else you may say, I'm satisfied Joe's call is genuine inspired—why, to build up such a turnout as this, first fifteen minutes of a healing service—you have to give the devil his due. I've since wrote the *Reader's Digest* about it.

I was beyond myself all of a sudden. I was turned two ways at once—pleased as punch on how good the Glory Road was rolling along, but dying to get my hands on Joe Crittenden at the same time. I couldn't make a move till there was some letup in the hallelujahs, but just wait for a little lull in the procedures to get *my* two cents' worth in.

Joe pointed a finger to the back of the tent.

"The Spirit is HERE with US toNIGHT!"

Everybody looked around expecting to see Jesus. So did I, I admit.

"The sick and wore out be PRAISEDaBILLabillabilla-billabba!"

He flung hisself to his knees and foamed and give messages in the unknown tongue. Joe actually had a cleft palate (what they call a harelip) up to age six and a half where they did an operation on him, which is like splitting a crow's tongue so's he can talk. The operation was divine inspired, and Joe experienced hallucinations all the time he was under ether, of Heaven and meeting Jesus. He said you'd be surprised—the pearly gates look like cotton candy and Jesus carries a briefcase.

But I had inspirations of my own, and my bile came back up on me. I couldn't no longer stand the sight of Joe kneeling down in that shiny suit, knowing what I know—and I all of a sudden just up and tore down that aisle myself, my teeth shut tight on my Spearmint gum and shaking my fist at you-know-who. Believe you me, I stirred sawdust.

But for all my smoke and brimstone, I got complete drowned out in Sweet Jesuses, hallelujahs, and Amens. Folks took me for just another sinner looking for salvation like them. I saw where Joe saw me out of the corner of one eye, and I busted through the crowd to get at him.

By then Little Sister'd popped off her throne and come for me, little pink hands and arms outstretched for her momma, but Joe (still kneeling where he was) held onto her halo and held her back. To multiply insults with injuries I got my slacks caught in the spokes of that fat man's wheelchair, and if he'd accidental started his motor I could've got ground into sausage meat. Lucky he didn't —but I wouldn't tear loose for love nor money, so I had to content myself to yell bloody murder to all concerned.

"THIEF! Damn KIDnapper! I want some alimony support or MY CHILD back!"

People started looking at me. I had made my point.

Joe must've give some kind of signal for the organ to let loose, for it did, like thunder. Then Joe yelled out over top of the organ and everybody else:

"My friends in CHRIST JEsus, we have here before the Temple, a desper-ate sinner down in the primary magnitudes of iniquity!" He meant *me,* the slick conniver. He pointed down to where I was trying to crawl up a sawhorse. "An admitted *thief* and a *kid*napper begging the Almighty God for forGIVEness in the hopes of e-ventual redemption, and dear Little Sister—our angel on earth—will kindly (come forward, sweetheart) will kindly administer the miraculous touch of salvation to this unfortunate lost lamb bleating in the wilderness, and may God's bountiful fount of ever loving forgiveness flow. . . ."

One whole leg of my slacks got ripped off in the wheelchair, but I was on my way scrambling onto higher ground (as the hymn goes) and got all the way up one of the front sawhorses, gripping the plank platform for dear life, when Little Sister wiggled out of her daddy's arms and went and leaned over me with her King James Bible (and the meanest smile) cracked my fingers with the holy testament. I let loose and fell over backwards to shouts of *Sweet Jesus!* and *Christ be praised!* and next thing I knew it was the opening notes of the Invitation Hymn and I was stampeded down in the sawdust under a ton of braces and crutches and orthopedic shoes.

III

After I limped out I lucky got a taxicab on 27th Avenue and told him to wait while I redid my facial to try and hide a split lip and the beginnings of a black eye. I'd been fit to be tied all night, but I sure boiled over sitting in that cab. My head was so full of hornets my heartbeat almost got the best of me. But I finally calmed down and recognized it was no way to deal with Joe Crittenden, so I turned cold-blood as a black widow. It so happened I was carrying my new white plastic handbag that I picked up on sale in Lemon City, three ninety-eight, just big enough to hold an ice pick. I had scores to settle that called for assault, and you cannot handle a rattlesnake with eyebrow tweezers.

While I was at it, I'd sure teach Miss Fancypants (Little Sister) what the Bible means when it says Honor thy Mother and to not try another stunt like she tried on me onstage.

So me and the taxi bided our time till we saw the gospel tent empty out, then we tailed the Salvation Caravan—that was Joe's name for him and his Chrysler, and the Mack truck—all the way to Miami Beach to the newest brand-new streamlined hotel called the Chateau de Sable. It was all stainless steel and glass you could see through to the ocean with famous French statues lined along the driveway, half-naked, but that never bothered the Caravan—they drove right in. The doorman wore an old-time French general's uniform and expected a tip.

IV

I tried to get up to their room by telling a bellboy I was a girl reporter from the *Miami Herald,* but the bellboy went over to the front desk and the front desk called up and Joe must've said no reporters (or the bellboy told them I was only wearing one-legged slacks) because the front desk said no. I anyway at least found out they were located in the Antibes Suite, fifteenth floor, living high on the hog. One thing I learned from that private detective that got drunk in Copper Hill: for every front door that slams shut in a person's face, a back door is liable to be left unlatched.

Poking around behind a tinfoil palm tree looking for the Lady's Room, I found a fire-exit sign and a set of stairs leading up. Fifteen flights climbing won't do a person's bunions no good, but it does give your varicose veins some circulation. When I came out into the hall I knew I was on the right floor on account of there was Uncle Sam standing in their doorway doing guard duty.

Now, Uncle Sam is Joe's former prizefighter brother that quit the ring and went into wrestling to get on TV and got both ears chewed off. He looks like a teddy bear (without ears) but is more like a bulldog if he don't like your looks. He don't happen to like mine, but I'm mutual. I got hold of the facts about him being mixed up with gangsters in Newport, Kentucky, and I've twice wrote the FBI anonymous letters to try and get him deported back to Tennessee where he was born, but they never deported him.

I knew I couldn't get past Sam, but I also knew he had

kidney trouble from being wrestled around below the belt and went a lot to the bathroom.

Right then Little Sister slipped out the door with a fistful of nickels and dimes (collection money, you get a lot of silver), and Uncle Sam made a grab for her. Well, she's naturally slipperier than some punch-drunk palooka, so she easy got out from under him and run around the corner by the elevators. That dumb ox took off after her and saw where she was burying nickels in the sand urn.

"Don't do that, Sister baby, people spit in there."

"Shut up, stoop," says Sister. You had to give her credit for comebacks.

I see my chance to sneak into the Antibes Suite behind everybody's back, so did, and nobody the wiser.

It was three connecting rooms together and Joe in the next-door one, I knew, where the Stock Market Report was playing, which is Joe's favorite radio show. I kept the safety catch on my pocketbook open, where the ice pick was, in case Sam came in sudden. There was collection money all around in piles according to nickels, dimes, quarters, and halves—but I never touched a penny of it. What I did do was I went over to the dresser and poked through the drawers and rifled around in Joe's socks and papers looking for evidence.

I come across the following items: a pack of home-remedy labels for Heart-Eze (a home remedy Joe used to peddle); a baptism certificate for where Little Sister got baptized at Holyoak, Tennessee; a whole half a gross of "safeties" (Joe never lowered hisself to use condoms, they were for sale); printed dispensations from snakebite for the Church of Serpent Salvation in West Virginia; a summons summoning Joseph J. Crittenden to appear in the courthouse of Texarkana dated July 12, 1969, which was the year Joe sold corn liquor dressed up in embalming-fluid bottles and came within an inch of getting put on the chain gang. And such stuff. What I was mainly interested in was things I never laid eyes on before, like: Joe's tenderfoot badge from Boy Scout Troop 10 of Gravelpit, North Carolina, and his Dishonorable Discharge papers. (He can never be in the war again, or work in the PO.) But that's Joe for you, tenderfooted and dishonorable both.

Then my permanent wave like to fell out when I come across a Tri-State Insurance policy for a certain Miss Clara Joy Sims to the tune of ten thousand dollars, and double indemnities for accidental death! My eyes bugged out of my head and I tried to hold in my heartbeat. Squinting, trying to make out the fine print (there wasn't even a burial clause), I was just getting to where it told the various kind of accidental deaths allowed—drowned, shot accidental, struck by lightning—when, Jesus save me! (oh, was I shook up!), a big hairy arm wrapped me up in a half-nelson around my Adam's apple, and started to squeeze!

In the dresser mirror I saw where Joe stood right behind me, choking the livers out of me—me, my makeup turning purple, but Joe, sober as a cucumber, looking like he was getting fixed to set Judgment Day and ask the congregation, *"Are you Ready?"*

"What you doing in them papers?"

He never allowed me breath enough to answer back. I just kind of gargled, pitiful.

"I'll teach you to rifle a person's private papers!"

He give me a squeeze that made me spit out my Spearmint. Then all of a sudden his mind changed off murder. He let loose his grip and threw me halfway across the room till I cracked into the money table and a whole pile of dimes sprinkled down on me where I was collapsed. I couldn't talk a word for the next ten minutes.

He stood over me spread-legged with a whole half a

bottle of Old Crow in his drinking hand (Joe always drinks direct from the bottle, he says, "If I catch anybody's trench mouth I want it to be my own"), and all he was wearing was his silk pants to his suit and a pair of Scotch plaid suspenders. (Joe won't wear a belt, claims it causes constipation.) His hair was mussed from all the different exertions of a three-hour soul-saving revival—plus what he done to me—and his eyes all bloodshot from bourbon, or counting money or I don't know what, but he did look good-looking standing there that way like a picture star in a gangster movie. He's turning a mite white-headed over the ears, and claims he caught a hernia from creek baptizing (he drowned an old lady once, accidental, but she weighed two sixty-five and was sopping wet) but I don't care what anybody says, Joe's a fine figure of a man for age forty-three.

He went and shut the dresser drawer and turned off the stock market report and come back to me and fixed a squinty eye on me where I was still heaving for breath.

"Now let's you and me have ourself a little talk." He took a drink. "First place, what got into your bird brain to come busting into my revival like you did and upset the works screaming your head off about Little Sister and alimony? I'll teach you alimony, woman. I'll teach you some alimony you wish you never heard the word."

I couldn't do nothing but rub my throat and slobber.

"What ever got into you to come back in the second place? Figured we got rid of your evil influence back in Tennessee when you went whoring around with the Optimist Club."

I shook my head no, meaning I never got mixed up with no club, only one Optimist.

"Alimony? I'll teach you some alimony, you heathen Freemason-lover." He took another slug.

I finally got my blood back flowing again, and my breath:

"You—run out—on *me*!"

He kicked my shin so hard I like to passed out. "Don't counterdick *me*. Checked into the Whispering Pines with him, and Little Sister saw you. The both of you—you lying satan-in-skirts."

I was crying to beat the band, but it never made no impression on *him*.

He tilted his bottle for some more liquor but his eye lit on where I was still hanging onto the Tri-State papers. Bottle came down slow and deliberate. I wondered, was he going to hit me with it?

"You read that insurance policy?"

I nodded yes. His eyes went narrow and he got sly.

"You read anybody's name on it?"

I knew I had him strapped, so I could afford to get a little reckless. "I read the name of Clara Joy Sims."

His face gets stony as an Indian's when he's thinking. Oh, he was slick.

"I saved that girl from the wages of sin. She come into the campaign to sing for the Lord."

"That's awful heavy insurance for a soprano," says I.

He kept stony, kept thinking.

"Her momma wanted her to go into show business, and I said I'd do right by her."

"Oh?" says I. "I met her momma in Macon, Georgia, and was told different." I was breathing a whole lot better, and getting my dander up besides.

You should've seen Daddy Joe swallow that. He knew I knew plenty. So he goes into the bathroom and gets a toothbrush glass and pours me a nice-size drink of Old Crow and starts acting like a prince. "Here, take some. You look like something the cat drug in."

It did taste good after what I went through.

"It was a pity about that girl."

"A pity about what?"

"How she died. Unbaptized and all."

"Died?"

"Poor frail creature, she went and ate an overdose of jumbo fried shrimps in New Smyrna Beach, and died right out."

"Died?" was all I could say. I gagged on my drink.

"That's what I said. She was crazy for shrimps. Little Sister went and got her some from the Shrimp Bucket in New Smyrna Beach. Clara Joy went into convulsions that very same night."

I went a little bit off my head. "You went and *done* something to that child!"

But he took it calm, steady as a train track.

"Don't go getting no sinful ideas. Nothing of the kind. Ask the coroner. Coroner said natural causes. I tried to sue the Shrimp Bucket for selling ptomained shrimps, but their lawyers called for autopsy."

"Well, why didn't you autopsy then?"

"It was too late."

"Too *late.* You mean you cremated that poor thing?"

"Ashes to ashes, it's in your Bible. Besides, I don't hold with cutting up cadavers, on general religion principles."

V

Little by little I found out everything is pending, secondary inquest, lawsuit, insurance money, and all. While I was bent down picking up all them spilled dimes Joe bent down next to me for us to pray together, but I said nothing doing. I didn't want no prayers at a time like this. Then Joe offered me to come back to Jesus, and I told him I'd have to think it over.

I did take his offer of another drink though.

"Like a soft furry little rabbit," he says, starting to play around with my earlobe, which is one of my best features, both of us sitting cross-legged in dimes.

"You always was," he whispered. "—first time I ever laid eyes on you, I always . . . you always . . . you and me." Joe's got the nicest whisper when he's not shouting. Still whispering, he worked in a "morphamorpha-morphaditty-o," and hummed real low, like bees, "Amazing Grace," which is my favorite song (my Christian name is Grace), and reminded me of our early times together when all he was selling was Heart-Eze for a living, careless and easy back then as the breeze, and the whole state of Alabama our stomping grounds.

When he run out of Old Crow we switched to Canadian Club, though I've heard tell you shouldn't mix.

Yes, here I was back together with my common-law lover again, like back in Birmingham in back of his ratty old station wagon, mason jars of Heart-Eze stacked around us, when me and him first made up our future ambitions together—which didn't include no Little Sister, but Mother Nature had her say about that.

I quit picking dimes up and concentrated on my drink, and Joe laid his head in my lap. I let it stay there, for old times' sake. I'm sentimental, I admit. (I've got a loving nature deep down, for all my brass—so has Joe.) I turned dreamy and stroked Joe's salt-and-pepper sideburns with my little finger and he took hold of my knee where the leg of my slacks was ripped off.

Next think I knew I was in his bed in the air-conditioned bedroom, with a balcony.

Joe snores, but I'm used to that. I was too deep into my intentions to sleep anyway, and I was still wide awake when dawn came up. Sunrise caught me unawares. Not a peep out of a rooster—but then I remembered I was in Miami Beach. I didn't have the glimmers of a hangover, tucked between a pair of sheets with *Chateau de Sable* embroidered on the hem, pillowslips to match, feeling like a million dollars, all I could think of was the Lord works in mysterious ways indeed.

Start with little things first, like making Joe make me chairman of Holiness Solidarity. They'd nickname me Momma Grace and everybody'd stand up when I came late to Sunday school. I want a lot of things like that. Master Charge, and eat prime ribs in the same restaurants where the movie stars eat. All-aluminum suitcases that's lightweight for airplane rides (I've got no intentions to go on the Glory Road in the back of a Mack truck). Start doing the collection money myself, for I am good at arithmetic, and gradual take over the treasury. (If I catch Little Sister with her thieving hands in the collection again, I'll whip that kid till she can't sit down.)

My head swam from all the different possibilities.

First thing, get Joe to get me breakfast brought up on a tray. Scrambled eggs, grits, Virginia ham, and a strawberry malted milk—in a fancy hotel like that, all you do is call up. Then send a telegram to the New Smyrna Beach Police Department, anonymous, that Uncle Sam Crittenden is a known criminal that was acquainted with the diseased Clara Joy Sims to get Joe off the hook. We might collect that ten thousand yet.

I will start talking wedding bells the minute Joe wakes up. I always did want to get married in front of a justice of the peace, with *witnesses*. No use putting the wedding off—especially when a person knows what I know, and Joe knows it. (In the first place it would keep Little Sister from being a bastard—but that never cut no ice with Joe, he was born outside of wedlock hisself.) My main argument is a wife can't testify against their husband.

If I play my cards right (and keep off shrimps) my horoscope is going to be looking up from now on.

Gambler's Chances

MISTRAL all of a sudden let up on a Saturday afternoon. I had spent the whole entire morning counting my
money, making triple sure I had as much as I thought I
had. I was right in the middle of checking the insides of
my eyelids in the dresser mirror (just pink means anemia,
red means good blood—I was OK) when the wind went
off. I listened a minute to make sure. Mistral wind is a
steady nervous sound like a steam whistle and when it
finally lets up you go limp as a rag doll. I sat down on
the bed and scratched my back with a hairbrush and relaxed myself. My ears popped some like from high pressure or swimming-pool water, but I finally got all right.

Then I got all excited and got up and counted my money again.

So I took my guitar and my gear and took off downhill from Ys, walking, pocket money folded neat in my pocket, change rattling musical against my hip. Felt like Noah right after the flood, or rather, felt like I just got out of the army, or jail. On the road I jumped over tree branches that got blew down in the wind. One time I stopped to try and wash my face in a waterfall, but I got all wet trying. Took a bus in Grasse, took me almost all afternoon to get to Cannes. I kept feeling in my pocket where my money was and humming soft to myself: *I'm a rambler and a gambler and a long way from home.*

I figured to double that easy money of mine easy, but they wouldn't let me in the Casino because I didn't have a necktie on or because I was black, I never did know which. So I asked a taxi driver where the poor people did their gambling and he said get in. So I did.

I was right away sorry. He drove me way deep into the backwash of Cannes through tight streets I wouldn't trust in daylight, let alone night. What I could see of the houses was just high smoky-gray walls and nicotine-stained windows and busted drainpipes sagging down to the sidewalk. Not even a cat prowling curbstones down *those* streets, except us two cats, and the only light was the taxi lights. I was about to say never mind, just drive me back to where I come from, when the driver turned into a little pocket alley where it didn't even look like a cab would fit. That's where we stopped. I had to suck my belly in to squeeze me and my guitar through the cab door. Then a shadow of somebody slid up by the driver, and driver and Shadow whispered a minute. I wasn't liking this deal one bit. Wanted out. But I had a funny feeling if I got back in the cab the driver wouldn't've took me. How I ever get myself in such jigsaw puzzles, and dangerous? I stood sweating worried wondering how I could slide by out of the alley, but the cab blocked me off.

Shadow come up to me and asked me if I had an *américaine,* meaning an American cigarette, and I said no, which was the truth. Then he pointed his finger at a corrugated iron shutter and walked behind me all the way over to it. There was a door cut out of it that we went through.

I busted my shins on the staircase, but Shadow never even said sorry or tried to light a light. I knew I had to keep walking, Shadow breathing down my back—I had that cold feeling between my shoulder blades I was going to get a knife pushed in me any minute. He said *là-haut,* and that's where I went.

At the top of the stairs a door busted open and the biggest fattest mama of them all blossomed out of it. I took a breath and felt better right away, seeing her, see she was black to begin with and her hair rigged up in ivory curlers looked like wishbones. Rest of her was zebra-stripe gunnysack dress and beads made out of it looked like washers and a whole brass-knuckle set of glass diamonds catching the light from behind the door.

"Qu'est-ce que c'est?" she bellowed down to Shadow, deep croak like a man.

"It's an American," Shadow said back to her. I saw in the light that Shadow was black too.

When we got to the landing, fat mama from the Congo took my hand and like to squeezed the blood out of it, big bracelets dangling down looked like handcuffs.

"All exiles here," she said.

For a couple of minutes I couldn't see much for the smoke, and when Mama tried to take my guitar away from me to check it in the checkroom I said no thanks. But Shadow took it away from me anyway, and my duffel. Big bright light bulb hanging down on a cord. Paper hat for a lampshade. I watched where Mama put my stuff, back behind a fake-bamboo bar where there was a sign chalked up over a shelf of cognac bottles, *Nouveau Club Africain.*

All around me a whole convention of African delegates, all wearing cool French clothes of tight St. Germain pants and short-length padded-out jackets and those pointy typical Frenchman shoes with heels thick as boot heels. Everybody was sitting around low to the ground on straw hassocks or sofa pillows. Some just squatting there.

"All my boys," says Mama, waving her arm over the congregation, rattling her handcuffs. "What'll you have to drink?"

"Rien, merci," said I. I was afraid of what they'd put in my drinking glass.

But she went and got me a cognac anyway.

"Ten francs."

"Ten *francs?*"

Shadow eased up beside my elbow and said, "Private club." Mama smiled big and said, "All exiles here." So I dug down for my roll, surprised it was still there, and took off a ten.

Then Shadow took my roll away from me. I grabbed out for it back, but Shadow too fast for me. It was already disappeared, all my money, gone. I was going to argue for it, but I saw all those delegate faces looking up at me from the floor, and I shut up, outnumbered.

Mama gave me a handful of toothpicks.

"Chips," she says. Then she waddled over to the gambling ring and croaked, "Malagash!"

"Malagash here."

"Move over."

Malagash moved and made a space and Shadow threw a sofa pillow down for me to sit on. I tried to squat down without spilling my cognac. Man on my right said, "Dahomey, five years." "Malagash, seven*teen*," said Malagash. I didn't know what to say so I said, "United States of America, all my life."

A whistle went all around the room.

"That's a long time exile," Dahomey said.

"Définitif," said somebody.

"Presque éternel," Malagash said, and he went all sympathy and showed me a picture of his two stringbean girls in cotton sacks, back home in Madagascar.

"All exiles here," Mama declared, "game is open as of right now."

I saw the game was craps, and that's fine with me. I'm an old-time payday crapshooter from way back. I maybe win my guitar back.

Togo, eight years exile, had the dice, but he handed them across to me. Said, *"Vous êtes le champion."*

But there was six dice and I didn't know the damn game. And when I looked at the cubes I saw they were coal black and no dots. "Roll," said Shadow, so I rolled.

"You lose," Mama said. Shadow took four toothpicks away from me.

"But where's the dots? What's *win?*"

"Roll," said Shadow.

"No dots," Malagash whispered. "It's all position."

"What's my position?"

"Roll," said Shadow. So I rolled.

On my way out I asked for my guitar back and Mama gave it to me gladly, and my duffel.

"All exiles here," she said, *"mais vous êtes le champion."*

I could see good enough now to see the walls where

there was pictures pinned up from the brown sections of a whole lot of different newspapers—famous national bigshots from all over, including half a dozen kings and one queen and a couple of presidents. All white people, too, but looking a little suntan from being in the brown section. I recognized most everybody.

I asked if I could get a refund on my cognac since I never drank any of it. Mama laughed fit to die. Shadow smiled.

"Never mind about being losers, son," Mama told me. "We all be winners by and by."

I doubt it. Nobody tells you the game.

"It's all for the Movement," Shadow says. He never said what movement.

"All exiles here," Mama said, squeezing some more blood out of my hand. "All my boys." Handcuffs rattled. Her boys wave me good-by.

I saw there was little spikes nailed into everybody's heart up in those pictures. They might as well've put my picture up there with the rest of them, busted toothpick in my teeth, crucified through my moneybelt. I was broke again, but I at least never got cut up with Shadow's or nobody's blade. I had my guitar back too.

"*Bonne nuit.*"

"*Au revoir.*"

"Roll," says Shadow to Malagash.

My cab was still waiting for me in the alley, faithful as a sheep dog. I looked and I had just enough chickenfeed change to pay my way back downtown. We went back the same streets as before and now they didn't look half bad, all the danger gone, since I was broke. I didn't mind traveling that country anymore at all.

Then I went on up to the Casino and hung around the driveway waiting till a bunch of big-winged birds come out smiling winners and smelling of money. I played them "Gambler's Chances" and "Eighter from Decatur" and "Money Talks." They stopped and noticed me and listened. Whitest people you ever saw. *White?*—you couldn't beat them for whiteness, and one little guy wearing a white suit on top of it. White Suit took up a collection and I made enough stake to play pinball machines till the cafés closed and that night I stayed all night with a whore called herself Lily and wore a sailor hat to bed. Adding up the morals and the discounts of it, there's a Sunday school lesson in there somewheres and as soon as I figure it out I'm going to remind myself to remember it.

The Snowbird

HE CONSULTED with snowbirds and file cards in eight-by-fourteen feet of office space called A-1 Personnel & Employer Consultants: green metal army surplus desk and dented file cabinet, telephone, one single window looking out on a restaurant parking lot—the only consultant was Donald B. DeGraf himself, alone. He shared a washroom with Real Estate across the hall.

A big man, DeGraf got his clothes from Greater Miami Men's Comfortwear (*We "Suit" the Larger Sizes*). He slit the sides and backs of his shoes for ventilation; he wore sponge pads in his armpits. One entire desk drawer was full of handkerchiefs. He tucked them one after another into his collar under the fleshy roll of chin, like napkins—and later washed them out himself, in the wash-room, and hung them out the window to dry: a string of wet pennants flying over the tops of automobiles parked below.

For all the olive-drab scrappy officeware at A-1, De-Graf's swivel chair was a work of art: custom-made of airplane aluminum with contour padding, ball-bearing joints, an H-shift gear shift for the adjustable seat and rubber-shod wheels instead of rollers. During the snow-bird season he seldom got out of it.

A-1 was ideally located, like a duck blind, across the street from Florida State Unemployment. Flocks of snow-birds flew across all summer. Florida Unemployment checked them in, classified them A through L, M through W—but a claim took maybe a month to process, and that first compensation check was weeks away; snowbird's prior home state might not even back his claim, or a hospital was where careless claimant last worked—hospitals did not qualify. Then DeGraf got them. Even a snowbird has to eat.

The decoy word was *Personnel,* a perfect bird call. Set yourself up as an employment agency, or use the crude word *job,* and you collect all the drifters, the dishwashers. Personnel Consultants brought down and bagged a slightly higher-class bird: waitresses, beauticians, and bell-boys. And, with a name like A-1, you got listed first in the Yellow Pages.

One of these days DeGraf was going to put an air-conditioner in, but right now an electric fan with rubber blades stirred the scorched air while DeGraf sat tilted back in second gear watching the frosted-glass window-pane of the office door, waiting.

"Parakeets was when it all started collapsing down around us when I failed to cash in on the parakeet craze after Herbert warned me my own mother warned me and everybody said it was going to last and last but I wouldn't listen once I made my mind up and stocked dalmatians even after my sister-in-law came down from Chicago and claimed Chicago was wild over parakeets everybody wanted one and the pet shops couldn't keep up with the orders for one well Herbert said you're crazy if you don't stock parakeets and my own mother warned me hoop-skirts'll be back in style before dalmatians but do you think I'd listen to some sense once I make up my mind stubborn is my middle name and I figured parakeets would all of a sudden just die out or else the government would ban them for parrot fever but they didn't and it got so bad you couldn't *give* dalmatians away and everybody knows if you can't sell the pups pretty soon you've got full-grown animals on your hands to feed just after we'd built up to be the nicest well-known pet shop in Indianapolis till parakeets came in and ruined us and I think that's what finally aggravated Herbert's allergies to where I said all right you're a sick man and I'm a ruint woman let's pull up stakes but then Momma died and that delayed us I don't know if you know what funerals cost anymore but after we sold the pet shop for peanuts to what it was worth and buried Momma all that was left to pull up stakes with was chickenfeed to come down to Miami and start life all over again fresh at our age with Herbert's allergies but I did have some of the cutest dalmatian pups you ever laid eyes on before everything went bust. Don't talk to me about parakeets."

"Not parakeets," said DeGraf, "goldfish." He had selected a three-by-five index card from the file and dealt it to the bird lady, face down, on the blotter. "Here's a fresh start for you. Ninety-eight fifty a week. Includes a good hot meal at the lunch counter."

"What kind of goldfish? I mean, what doing?"

76

"—just yesterday they had milk-fed shoulder of veal with mashed potatoes and garden peas. I was there for lunch myself, that's the kind of meals they serve. One of the nicer higher-class ten-cent stores on Flagler, selling goldfish."

"I used to have my own store. Goldfish? I never . . . I don't know."

"We never know till we try." DeGraf shifted gears and settled deeper into the swivel chair. "To be perfectly frank, and I make no bones about this, *if* you should be hired"—and the word *if* hung there a moment between them—"*if* you should be lucky enough to get this position you can count yourself among the exceptional ones. One in a thousand."

"One in a what? I mean, lucky how?"

She was shaking her beak back and forth I-don't-know, I-don't-know. She was a bird all right, he said to himself, watching her pluck the lint from her blouse front; picking nits, he thought, from her fine feathers.

"Let me be absolutely perfectly frank with you about how the way things are down here. The employment situation. In a nutshell, well, the employment situation, for people like yourself, from somewhere else, from somewhere up north, for people we call—rather, the residents down here call"—and the word *residents* hung there a moment between them—"well, the *residents* have got a name for those kind of people. They call them, to be absolutely frank, snowbirds."

"Snow what?" She lowered her head until the great beak sank out of sight. "I mean, I had my own pet shop. We came down here, like I said, for a fresh start."

They come down, DeGraf said to himself, calling themselves pioneers. *Pioneer* is the word they start out with, but when they get down here there's a colder word for them.

"Before," she said, "I was a resident myself, in Indianapolis. I mean, you can't be a resident till you live down here can you, right off the bat?"

But DeGraf was in first gear now, accelerating, and the chair shot across the brief splintery floor space between them. She was startled, fluttery, ready to fly—but trapped with the swivel chair between her and the door, as he rolled up to her with an A-1 contract form and a ballpoint pen in his hand. He was reminded of a cockatoo's crest when the pointed tufts of her dyed-orange hair appeared to curl forward in fear. Her bare arms in the cheap sleeveless blouse were suddenly pebbled with chicken flesh. DeGraf braked the swivel chair just short of the painted bird claws showing through a pair of open-toed huaraches.

She blushed under her feathers, but signed her foolish name, saying, "I just hope I don't have to wait on a lot of colored people."

He spun around in his chair at the sound: a young girl had slipped into his office through the door left open by the bird lady. Another snowbird, but that was nothing to be surprised about—this was the season.

Where do they come from? DeGraf asked himself, and the answer was: anyplace north, turning a little cold, looking a little grim in the first gray rain. Last summer was this girl's first summer to wear a bikini, and now she wants to wear one year-round.

A pretty thing, he thought, as he handed her an Address & Next-of-Kin card to fill out, and a Personal History form—but by now Personal Histories were all the same, and that form might as well be phased out. Twenty-two years in the swivel chair had given DeGraf a personal knowledge of Personal Histories. A Personal History form was for the birds; he never read them: he read faces, then shuffled index cards, consulting.

The girl was bent over her ballpoint. Nice little hand, DeGraf noticed, with a nice wristwatch her daddy probably rewarded her with at high-school graduation. Her legs were neatly crossed. Very nice legs, thought DeGraf, and he could see them in a drum majorette's saucy pleated skirt. They were sweet and tender cheerleader's legs: last year she was leaping up and down on those legs yelling riot songs to the football team. But right now the legs were tightly knotted together, and a strict job-hunting handbag lay in her lap.

She wore a gold chain around her neck, tucked in above the top button of her virginal white blouse. No doubt her high-school hero's gold football hung at the end of that chain, suspended between those twin delicacies: the doubtlessly perfect breasts that only her high-school boyfriend (and possibly one or two others on the team) had touched.

High school behind her, she had come to Miami to be an airline hostess, DeGraf decided—or a fashion model. The fledglings were all alike, looking for a share of glamour in this humdrum workaday world. But Donald B. DeGraf had long years of experience bringing teenage dreamers down to earth.

He waited for her to recite past failures and future hopes to him, but she sat silent with her unblinking owl eyes staring across the desk into his. Like a violinist, he replaced the sweaty handkerchief at his chin with a fresh one from the desk drawer, then sank back into the chair's reclining second gear, saying, "Well, I suppose you came down here to be a stewardess on one of our major airlines."

"No. No planes, please. I get airsick."

Strange, he thought, a snowbird unwilling to fly.

"Or maybe you left home with modeling in mind."

"Not me. I just want a job."

DeGraf sat up straight. Here was a bird of a different

feather, she was a species apart. Her great green eyes stared innocence at him: they were limpid pools that maybe quarterbacks tumbled into—but not DeGraf.

"You want to go into television, I know what you want. You want to be an exhibition swimmer, or water-ski for a living. Maybe you think you'll manage an exclusive dress shop for wealthy matrons or interior-decorate seventeen-room villas on Key Biscayne. Tell me, just what kind of ex*perience*"—and the word *experience* hung there between them—"what real *experience* have you had?"

"I never worked before."

"Exactly," said DeGraf. "No experience."

"To get a job you're supposed to have experience, but to get experience you have to first get a job."

DeGraf smiled. Hearing the old sweet bird song, he reclined into second again. Idly he took up the deck of index cards and shuffled through, searching the proper pigeonhole for this pigeon. "Elevator operator," he announced, and tossed the card out, face down on the blotter. "One of the higher-class hotels on the beach."

"Elevator what?"

"—older-type, newer-rich clientele. You wear a snappy little uniform with brass buttons and a bow tie. The tips, they tell me, are something to write home about. These people have got money to burn. Six-foot-six Texans who left their wives home in Dallas, and Cubans who got their money out of Havana before Castro snatched it. The famous inventor, I forget his name, the one who found out how to make breakfast cereal out of seaweed, keeps a penthouse suite all season."

"Elevator operator? I get motion sickness."

"—*if* you should be lucky enough to get this position."

"I never said I wanted it. I'm thinking it over. I'm trying to picture myself cooped up in an elevator all day."

When they start thinking it over, when they start

shaking their silly heads I-don't-know, it is high time to clip their wings for them.

"Let me be absolutely perfectly frank with you," De-Graf began—but Green Eyes was not listening.

She bent her fingers delicately to see what the bus ride had done to her fingernails. She looked out of the narrow window to where a string of handkerchiefs hung drying. She yawned.

She sat a firm perch, he had to admit; but he was, after all, the almighty birdwatcher. It was DeGraf who held a full house of index cards and rationed out the birdseed in this world. Still, by the time he came to the word *snowbird,* he was in a desperate sweat, and his voice was pitched higher than he intended.

When he finished, she simply said, "You're the bird, if you ask me."

DeGraf went around in his swivel chair, a slow spin—contemplative, not stunned. When the chair stopped he closed his eyes to keep his head from spinning on. Then he reached a shaky hand into the drawer full of handkerchiefs.

Maybe he moved in too close, too slowly—or that last fumbling change of handkerchiefs had thrown his timing off—because her wide unblinking eyes surveyed the swivel chair's approach, and she was waiting for him when he got to her. His brakes failed and their knees bumped. She placed one firm hand flat against his heaving chest, and with the other hand yanked at the gold chain around her neck. A tiny gold cross dangled from the chain, instead of a football.

DeGraf threw the chair into reverse and scuttled backwards, crablike—like the vampire in a horror movie. Then he spun the chair a half-circle to the file drawer where he kept a bottle of rye whiskey wedged between the cards. As he drank he heard the purse go shut, and when he turned she was gone. Where she had been sitting an unsigned A-1 contract lay on the floor, a dirty sheet of paper at the bottom of his birdcage.

"Wellsir first the *first* retaining wall went and there went my garage foundations and I could've kicked myself for forgetting to remember to test your hillside first for drainage but I've learnt my lesson since believe you me and when the second wall went I swore on a stack of Bibles if ever I built anywheres on a slant someplace I want to know where the water comes through first and second if there's any highway referendums on the ballot because where I built the county voted yes and they put a road through that cut in above my house and I got the drain down my backlot which loosened up my underbeams till you couldn't cross across the kitchen for a drink of water without the whole floor shook but I'm a builder by trade a *builder* by damn a born builder if there ever was one and a crackerjack carpenter to boot and I'm a son of a gun if I couldn't build better than builders build nowadays if I do say so myself with your electric saws whatever became of good old-fashioned elbow grease and your solid so-called reinforcement concrete it may be solid but who wants to live in all-concrete unless it's a mausoleum or your prefabrications made out of sawdust either might as well live in a cardboard outhouse and I never got back a word of complaint in forty years building other people's houses but my luck seemed like it run out when I went and built one for myself for it washed right out from under me the first hard spring rain my two and a half retaining walls and all."

DeGraf was lying back in third gear, like a stretcher case, while Mr. Carpenter, a carpenter, confessed. That slug of whiskey had set off DeGraf's colitis: he felt unpleasant things happening inside him—also, he had changed three dripping handkerchiefs since Mr. Carpenter came in.

It was lucky the telephone rang, for DeGraf was not up to talking to a ruined carpenter right now. He reached out for the phone without sitting up, without looking.

"A-1."

"DeGraf? Blakey, over at the Chateau de Sable. That elevator job you had us down for? Forget it, we filled it already."

DeGraf sat up.

"Ten minutes ago this girl walked in the door, just right, just what we need."

"What girl?" DeGraf demanded, trembling.

"This *girl,* she just walked in, uniform fits her nice and everything. We hired her. So forget the elevator job you had us down for. What we need now is a night watchman."

"That girl. The one you hired. Tell me something. I'm curious. What were her legs like?"

"Legs? What do you mean, *legs?*"

"Was she wearing a wristwatch her daddy gave her for graduation?"

"What do you mean? What're you talking about?"

"And a gold chain. Did she have on this gold chain around her neck? I'm just curious, that's all. I was just wondering."

"I don't know what she had on for chrissake. She's wearing an elevator uniform right now is all I know."

"Listen, do me a favor. Take a look and tell me what color her eyes are."

"Green," said Blakey. "I don't have to take a look. Now will you forget the elevator girl a minute and listen? What we need is a night watchman. One twenty a week and we pay his Blue Cross. You know, for the side door, for employees only. Check time cards and not let anybody in except deliveries. It can be an old guy—but *active,* you know."

"Night watchman," said DeGraf, distracted. "You need a night watchman."

"That's what I said. Jesus, you sound like you're under ether." And Blakey hung up.

He could take her to court. A nice little lawsuit would wipe that smile off her face. He'd put her in every blacklist in the book. She had turned up the index card on the blotter—nobody ever did that—and saw Chateau de Sable written on it.

Cheerleader? Graduation gift? She stole that wristwatch from her roommate. She never had a boyfriend on the football team, she was some gangster's gun moll. Vice queen, police informer, drug dealer, whore . . .

He could take her to court—but where did that get you? It only got you in deeper with those green eyes, maybe victimized again, maybe laughed at. Let Blakey have her. Blakey, the bell captain at the Chateau de Sable —he'd take her home with him tonight. A nice dose, that's what Blakey would get out of it. She'd take him and the Chateau de Sable for plenty, plenty. DeGraf could picture Blakey getting taken.

Well, surely, one mistake, at least, allowed in twenty-two years. But look at Mr. Carpenter. One mistake and there he sat cracking his big arthritic knuckles, nervous, waiting to hear the snowbird song. All his life was bad news now since his house washed down a hillside onto the Louisville & Nashville tracks. Not a contractor in all of Kentucky would trust him with a hammer again.

"Let me be absolutely perfectly frank with you," De-Graf began, "—*if* you should get this position . . ."

If? Mr. Carpenter pinched his red beak and blinked his watery blue eyes. A beer drinker, thought DeGraf, an old bird sliding downhill with his house. He wore a sporty tie knotted too thick for his denim workshirt collar, trying to look years younger than his stone-white hair. A railroad timepiece ticked like thunder in his shirt pocket. He planned to get back into the building trade, back on his feet—Florida was too flat for what happened back home to happen here. The old man had come down for a fresh start. A snowbird he was, and wanted to be a carpenter again—but suddenly, as if the force of gravity depended upon it, DeGraf needed to make a night watchman out of him.

Story Hour

THE REASON the trees all died around the court-house was on account of Eljay. Eljay was a nigger that went up one time and sawed the dead limbs off the live oaks, only he sawed too much. He also forgot to spray the arborvitae hedge, and it is full of worms. The tree trunks are still standing around for no good reason with their dead limbs sticking up in the air like amputees.

The whole town is backwards like that. No wonder they moved the county seat away from Watershed to Williamstown. Court trials don't amount to a row of beans anymore: a lawsuit once a year whether somebody's bullpen is astraddle somebody else's boundary or not; Red Circle Stores or Harmony Hardware work up a shoplift or a nonpayment now and then. When Watershed was still county seat, and had a circuit court judge once a month instead of just a justice of the peace, it was different. There was a lively murder trial once over a farmer that stove in his own field hand's head, with a mattock. But that is long forgotten, and now hardly anybody even remembers how it turned out. All Jimbob went to the courthouse for anymore was Story Hour.

Whenever Jimbob passed through the courthouse grounds he thought about wartime on TV and would rather be watching it than going to Story Hour. The dead live oaks with their limbs cut off reminded him of a marine on TV that stepped on a booby trap and was interviewed. The man would collect over eighty percent disability from the VA and was set for life. The only reason Jimbob went to Story Hour in the first place was his momma made him.

"Allrightsir. No Story Hour, no TV. You can just take a restful siesta for yourself."

"No thanks," said Jimbob. "A nap is worse than Story Hour."

The astronauts were going to the moon again that afternoon, and if their spacecraft happened to blow up on TV (so what, we were already way ahead of Russia) he would hate like the dickens to miss it. He figured he was already missing the blast-off on account of being on his way to Story Hour.

People said the courthouse was going to rack and ruin, and Jimbob saw where they were right. Weeds grew right up out of the flagstone steps. The whole front lawn was more crabgrass and dandelions than anything. That was Eljay's fault, the janitor. He was already asleep at 3 P.M. when Jimbob came by. Stretched out on a warped closet door somebody had hired him to plane down, on two sawhorses. His tin cup was on a watch chain attached to one strap of his overalls dangling down swinging under the door, empty. He always carried his own cup on a chain so he wouldn't lose it. In case somebody offered him a drink. Naturally he could not drink out of the same bottle with a white man.

Watershed may be dry, but the next county is not—and there are more bootleggers around town than you can shake a stick at. Jimbob saw an empty pint bottle on the door with Eljay. Bootleggers will sell to niggers, anybody. Eljay was known to be drunk half the time and the other half asleep. Right now he was both.

(Eljay's only sober memories were when they let him be bailiff and run for Cokes for the jury and take up spittoons after a trial. He was the only nigger bailiff in Tennessee. Then they went and changed the county seat to Williamstown, and Watershed ended up with only a justice of the peace. So Eljay gave up trying, and took to drink.)

Jimbob stepped into the courthouse out of the heat. There sat Miss Poindexter in the judge's seat, as per usual.

Miss Poindexter read. They put her in charge of the library since she went and wore a NEVER button and got out of schoolteaching. All the library was, was a closet next to the jury box. It was full of old books a lady gave to Watershed when she died, a lot of *Little Colonel*s and *Life* and old back issues of *Kiwanis Magazine*s with silverfish in the pages from how damp it gets. Also a stack of half-burnt hymnals from when the Cherry Log church caught fire and they bought new ones. There was a stack of *Perry Mason*s, too, but Miss P would not allow anybody under fifth grade to read them. Jimbob would not have got caught dead in the library except his momma made him.

His momma felt sorry for Miss Poindexter. Miss Poindexter was peculiar, and never got married. The only thing anybody could think of for a not-too-bright and not-married lady to do was teach school, so she did it. Jimbob had her himself in second grade. She was a stretched-out type of woman on the order of a telephone pole. Her folks were all tall people, and she took after them. Her teeth were nice, and her own, but big. She had never in her life dipped snuff, which left them whiter than most. She always tucked her ears up inside her tight hair to where you never saw them. She had little-bitty eyes and glasses. Jimbob did not know if she never married because she was peculiar or she was peculiar because she never got married.

When Miss Poindexter took to schoolteaching, Jimbob's momma said, "I do believe that woman's found her niche in life at last." But if you asked Jimbob, she was no genius at schoolteaching. He half the time stuck an *Action Comics* in his geography when he had her, and she never knew the difference. He did memorize his times tables off Miss Poindexter—or was it some substitute from Chattanooga?, for Miss P was out a lot with heart trouble and the heat. That was before they Integrated. And Miss Poindexter switched her cameo she used to wear for a NEVER button.

A long time ago, about World War II, nearly every nigger in Watershed went to Cincinnati to work at Wright's until all that was left now was one black family in the whole county. That was Eljay and his woman Pearl —and they weren't even the least bit married. Pearl used to take in washing at a penny-a-piece (be it sheet or handkerchief), so naturally the women all sent sheets till she got smart and charged a nickel. They had this little girl, Trellis. Jimbob doubted if Trellis ever saw the insides of a schoolhouse till Integration came along. They sent a marshal all the way from Memphis just to put Trellis in school.

The marshal had to sit in a teeny-tiny second-grade seat like Trellis, and not smoke.

What Miss Poindexter decided to do was turn her back on Trellis and the Law of the Land both. Jimbob was in second grade himself, and saw her do it. She wouldn't teach Trellis to spell *cat*. And pinned on a NEVER button where her cameo used to be, for good measure.

The whole town said she was a mighty plucky female to buck the government like that. Jimbob's momma said she put the KKK to shame. The KKK talked a lot about burning a cross downtown, but they never got around to it. Jimbob never saw such a yellow Klan as Watershed's was. When he got old enough he was going to join the White Knights in the next county, which was a whole lot higher-class.

Then this marshal went and reported Miss Poindexter's NEVER button to Memphis. She got her picture in the papers but lost her second grade. The school board had to back down to the government and take her off school-teaching. They couldn't think of anyplace to put her except in the library instead.

She still wore her NEVER button to Story Hour.

So you could have knocked Jimbob over with a feather when he eased into the big old dark courtroom and who should be sitting in the witness stand, big as brass? It was Trellis. It looked like even Story Hour was getting integrated.

Jimbob tried to slink down to about angleworm size, to where nobody that knew him would know he was Integrated in the same room with Trellis, without a marshal. The only soul in sight besides her was Miss Poindexter, in the judge's seat, sitting as relaxed as a TV weather report.

It was a puzzle. In the first place, there wasn't the least need to drag a nigger kid to Story Hour since her marshal long went back to Memphis a month ago. The school board already took a vote to just let Trellis keep on in second grade by herself a few years till she got wore out or old enough to quit, one. That was all the Integration, they said, anybody could put up with in one town.

(But it turned out it was Miss Poindexter herself that got Trellis to come! That is an idea of just how peculiar Miss Poindexter was.)

It was all cool and spooky in there, with the window shades rolled down against the afternoon sun and only one light lit up behind the judge's bench where Miss Poindexter was sitting to see to read by. She had a storybook already open to some story she was going to read. Jimbob had a good notion to hightail it home, for he figured she had never noticed him coming in. That was where he was wrong. She must have heard his tiptoes or something. She put on her glasses she wore to see with (she read without) and said, "Jimbob!"

He had been meaning to hunch down behind the last row of benches, but too late. She had the same type of voice of every retired schoolteacher there ever was, and sheriff.

"Just pleasesir step right up here in front where we're all nice and Integrated."

Jimbob was mortified, but he did it. At least he did not have to *sit* with any nigger. Trellis was up sitting in the witness stand, by herself.

Something he noticed when he got up front in the light was where the closet door was off on the closet over next to the jury box. That must have been the very door Eljay was laid out asleep on. The closet was the closet Miss

Poindexter kept the library in. Only it was all emptied out now. She had all her raggedy magazines and yellowy books piled up in the jury box, and piled up next to the closet with the door off was a stack of cinder blocks. There was even a tub of wet cement up there. Jimbob reckoned Eljay was told to fill in that old closet—but if he didn't quick sober up and get busy his cement was going to dry up on him.

"Boys and girls," said Miss P (but Jimbob didn't see any boys-and-girls to it, only himself and a nigger), "this afternoon we're a-going to read a lovely-special tale by Mr. Edgar Allan Poe, poet and Virginian."

Jimbob took a look at Trellis on her witness chair to see how she was taking to Integration. Not too hot. She was shiny as a tarbaby from the sweats, and her witness seat was too high for her. Pearl had put her into a big orange organdy sundress, with white sandals to top it off. The sandals didn't anywhere near touch the floor on account of how short-legged she was. She couldn't have budged if she wanted to, her dress was so stiff with starch.

" 'The Cask,' " said Miss P, " 'of Amontillado.' "

"Phooey," said Jimbob (but not out loud). He already saw that story on TV.

Miss Poindexter took her glasses off to see better. Her eyes were littler with glasses off than on.

" 'The thousand injuries of Fortunato I had borne as best I could . . .' " she started. But Jimbob's mind wandered off. All that story was about was two Italian fellas down in some cellar in Italy someplace. They had a feud on and one Italian buries the other one over some wine. What was the use of listening if you already knew how it turned out?

But somewhere in the middle of it Miss Poindexter stopped cold and said, "Boys and girls," again.

"Boys and girls," she said, "this afternoon instead of

only just reading out of our storybook like usual, in honor of our little darky visitor we've got with us today we're a-going to perform a nice pageant of Mr. Poe's tale."

To give you an idea of how peculiar Miss Poindexter was, here is what she dreamed up. She dreamed up for Trellis to go and stand in the closet and be Fortunato.

Trellis just looked at Miss P with her pullet-egg eyes as wide as they would go. So Miss P had to say it again: "Now if you'll please just step right over to that cupboard yonder, Fortunato, we'll get started on a right nice pageant for everybody."

Trellis naturally never budged. She was either too starched or too stubborn to. Miss Poindexter had to finally get up from the judge's bench and take hold of her orange organdy sundress by one wing, like something dead you take to the outhouse between two fingers. Trellis slid off her witness seat and walked stiff along next to Miss P with her starchy dress sounding like dry leaves when you step on them. They came right up to the closet together before Miss Poindexter let go. Trellis turned around still big-eyed as ever, and finally backed in slow, like a mule.

"Now Seen-yor Montresor, sir," (which was Jimbob) "will yousir be so kind as to take this here trowel"—and Jimbob came up and she handed him this trowel out of the wet cement—"and take and make up a nice neat row of blocks across the doorsill like in the story."

Well, he did it, but he was none too handy with a trowel. First three or four licks, Jimbob landed more cement on his big toe than on cinder blocks. And a cinder block to pick one up is no featherweight, either. But he finally got the hang of it and how to turn your cinder blocks sideways when you reach the end, to fit. He worked up a nice sweat his first five layers, though Jimbob would not likely win any medals for masonwork.

Jimbob finally got to where he could not reach his cinder blocks up that high anymore, and was going to get a chair out of the jury box to stand on, but Miss P quick snatched the trowel all excited out of his hand. For all her Sunday clothes and clean hands, she finished off his next row for him herself.

After that you could not get that trowel away from her for love nor money. Nothing for Jimbob to do but go and sit back down up front, bored stiff again. He would have given anything to be back home sitting in front of the TV. It never pays to miss a good show on TV. His momma was watching that time where Ruby shot Oswald, and just Jimbob's luck he was too little to watch TV in those days.

Miss P's hairpins were coming loose and Jimbob finally saw her ears for the first time in history. They were little-bitty like her eyes. Her wash-and-wear armpits turned into big wet moons of sweat before she was done. She shoved her last cinder block in with all her snow-white teeth showing. Her collar had come unfastened and that made her NEVER button hang down loose to where you couldn't read it.

Then, cool as a cucumber (but all kind of undone), she marched right back to her judge's bench and took up her Poe where she left off.

" 'I forced the last stone into its position,' " she read, and took a swipe at a stray hairpin hanging on a strand of hair hanging down to her storybook. " 'I plastered it up. Against the new masonry I re-erected the old rampart of bones.' "

(With a funny stomach Jimbob sneaked a look, but naturally saw no bones. It was only a pageant.)

Miss Poindexter took a dreamy look out in space without her glasses like she wasn't all there. The minute she said, " '*In pace requiescat!*' " and closed her book, Jimbob took off.

94

*   *   *

The late sun outside like to blinded him, but he could see old Eljay still laid out on that door dead drunk. He scooted on out a hole in the arborvitae hedge, which was pretty near *all* holes on account of the worms. He skidded down an embankment by the lumber mill to take a short-cut and be home before the "World News Roundup." The depot, when he went past, was all boarded up the way it always is. (The railroad put that depot in and then never laid track. They took a survey and said Watershed was way too steep for anything less than a diesel, and that was no run worth putting a diesel on for.) The whole town is backwards like that—Jimbob could hardly wait till he was sixteen and out of school and in the marines.

By going straight through the cannery he got home before his daddy did and got the best seat directly in front of the TV without having to look over somebody's shoulder. You had to sit up close to see anything. Watershed has got the worst TV reception in Tennessee. Put a fifty-foot antenna up and you will still get ghosts.

Hitchhike Ride to Miracleville

TWO SPANIARDS got in a fight over a woman and one got killed and his dead body threw under my viaduct where I used to go for lunch. Truckload of police came in from town.

Grape pickers said let's go see, and I didn't want to, but they all went so finally I did too and was sorry.

Whole string of cars pulled up in a ditch alongside the highway, crowd of pickers standing in the weeds by the creek bed, kids up on the viaduct looking down at the dead man. He'd got stabbed in the stomach, laying there awful in a puddle of blood.

Cops pushed through the mob with the murderer with them, and one of the cops carried the knife he did it with.

The murderer was just a kid, pale skin as a girl's, long dude sideburns and his black flashy hair slicked down with olive oil. He walked stony-faced between two cops, trying to look twenty years older than sixteen. His ma and a bunch of his kin came up right behind him, jabbering Spanish a mile a minute. Cops, murderer, and murderer's family made a ring around the dead man. This was France so the cops were talking French to him, but he didn't know French, just kept shaking his stony head I-don't-know. Everybody too excited for anybody to try and translate. Then the head cop tried to show—waving his arms, sign language, stabbing hisself—what he thought happened. But the murderer wouldn't even look at the body, just stared up at kids' feet hanging over the viaduct. The head cop finally got mad and grabbed the knife out of another cop's hand and waved it in front of the murderer's eyes. Murderer looked at the knife. Cop pointed the knife at the dead man and the murderer finally looked down at that bloody sight. Everybody else looked too. Then the murderer took to trembling all over, trembling terrible, till his legs caved in and he fainted.

He would've fell over flat on his face if he wasn't handcuffed to cops. His ma gave a scream and busted out crying. They had to carry him unconscious to the police truck. They carried off the dead man wrapped up in a tarpaulin.

For three nights after that, no sleep. Didn't even try to tune my guitar. It started in a rainy season and my tent leaked. Black man full of dark thoughts.

The grape picking was off, with the rain, and anyway most grapes already got picked clean before the murder. People took their tents down—big empty squares of dead grass where the tents and trailers used to be. A few old people hung around that lived there, out early of a morning looking for snails in the wet. Felt like a snail myself, getting no place, slow. When the last pickers packed up and went their different directions, so did I. On my way out saw where the blood was washed away under the viaduct from the rain. Sun started shining as soon as I hit the road.

Standing in the middle of a French superhighway with forty francs in my pocket clipped in a money clip with a U.S. penny soldered on it, says, *In God We Trust.* Stuck my thumb out at the first car that came spinning around the curve. Volkswagen, with two blue-eyed college boys in it and their fraternity sign painted on the car door. TT plates, meaning tourists. They passed me about seventy-five mph farting super hi-test backwards in my face.

About a dozen more cars went by, Dutch and Germans on their way to the Riviera, but they don't pick up blacks—get their seat covers dirty. Then finally another American came by, big shiny black car with a bald guy in it, and his wife. I do relish the sight of a hefty Cadillac heaving up to me with intentions to stop. That penny must've brought me luck, because somewhere out from behind a bunch of fancy baggage somebody (him or her, one) said, "Going as far as Lourdes, young man. Will that help you any?"

I didn't know how far Lourdes was, but it was in the right direction (out of here) so I said sure.

The man reached across the lady and pressed a button that clicked the back door open. Where was I supposed to sit? All their gear was back there, suitcases, Val-a-pacs, valises, briefcase, handmade baskets filled up with homemade souvenirs, Red Cross kit with a red cross on it, and a portable icebox filled up with Cokes and mineral water and No-Cal. There was a travel library set up along the window to where you couldn't see out of the glass, Michelin and Kleber guides to everyplace approved, plus books on where to eat, where to sleep, museums and what they cost, important cemeteries not to miss, main roads, detours, churches, mountain passes, holidays in holy places, walking tours, bicycle paths, how to speak every kind of language like a native, different seasons in their off-season, ten steps to amateur mountain-climbing, nationalities of different flowers and birds and cheese, famous people and where they died, and every kind of tip on how to stretch your dollar from one end of Europe to the other.

I piled what I could to one side and the man leaned over the back of his seat to scoop up cameras and light meters and field glasses, their straps all tangled together, to keep with him in the front seat. We finally worked it out to where if I put my elbows together and held my breath, there was a little squeezed-in place to one side of the back seat. I had to stick my guitar between my legs, but so what?—I was riding Cadillac, wasn't I?

"I'm Mrs. McHenry," the lady said, shaking her head no. She had the shakes real bad. "And this is Mr. McHenry. Where are you from?" Before I could say where, she said, "We're from Sylvan Hills, New Jersey. Not many people have heard of it because it's a private development. We have a lovely artificial private lake, Sylvan Hills Lake, which takes its name from the development."

"Some good fishing," Mr. Mac mumbled, and pressed the starter button to get us started.

"Oh, fish," Mrs. McHenry said. "Next thing the men will want is a golf course."

"Why not?" McHenry said, but she changed the subject to the house: "The house," she said, "is Tudor English."

"All the houses in Sylvan Hills are Tudor English," said he.

"There's a development code that you can't build unless you build Tudor."

She waggled a fingernail at me, warning me not to build if I didn't know my development code. This was going to be a longer ride than I first thought.

We swam out to the middle of the road and took over two lanes, just the least sweet-and-low hum—not a cough or a spit or a motor rev to be heard—maybe not even a motor down in there, she just ran on faith alone. Nobody said anything for minute while we all got our kicks out of that car.

The lady changed her regular glasses for sunglasses to see me better and give me the once over, sideways, shaking her head no, which got me nervous. Finally she gave up on studying me and relaxed back in her seat for a few kilometers. Only she couldn't relax. Her tic would go down to a tremble, but then a shiver'd come over her like somebody walking on her grave. She couldn't rest the least comfortable. As soon as she tried to settled down, the shakes took over and shook her out of position. Watching her made me uneasy myself.

Mr. Mac was all right. I mean he didn't shake. He was a very white guy dressed expensive for the road. One of those suits you can wash in your hotel room lavabo and hang it on the back of a chair to dry and put on next day. The chair back was still sticking out of the shoulders from last night's wash. He wore a vest and had a pen-and-pencil set in his vest pocket. His wristwatch could tell you what year it was, and the altitude. Hand-painted cocker spaniels on his necktie and a Shriner's clasp to keep the spaniels out of his soup. Chunky (but not too fat) in his wash-and-wear suit, soft pinky color, clean-shaved and smelling of after-shave fresh from this morning. I couldn't guess his age, or hers either—white people like that all look alike.

She was the talker for the two of them. She was trying to tell me something about some Father Finney took care of their mail back home, but the words came out jerky and she spit on the windshield stuttering something that started with *c*: "C-c-cance—c-c-canceled out the Chr-chr-chr—"

Mac broke in and said, "Canceled out the Sylvan Hills *Chronicle-Bulletin.*"

"If you let newspapers" (she took a breath and shook all over like a wet dog) "pile up on your porch, house-breakers will know you're gone, and break in."

Turned around to look me over again, see if I was a housebreaker. Then she remembered this was a long way from Sylvan Hills and forgave me with a smile. Anyway, Father Finney, and the cops, were keeping watch on her Tudor house.

"Our private police force picks up any strangers walking around Sylvan Hills at night for questioning, because what would anybody be doing walking around out there at night without a car?"

She took a coughing fit, shaking with it till the tears came. Mr. McHenry had to pull the Kleenex out of the box for her—he was good as gold with her, he treated her like a little child. He patted her knee *now, now* in the worst of it.

When she got through and her face dried off and some fresh lipstick on, she twisted around in her seat and said to me all of a sudden:

"You're Catholic, aren't you?"

Question took the wind out of me. Then I remembered that St. Christopher's medal hanging on a chain around my neck, medal a girl gave me at the grape pickers' camp. (Marie-Thérèse was her name, I called her Marie-T and we shared the same pup tent till her soldier-boyfriend showed up and she moved into his, but I got a week's loving and a St. Christopher's out of it.) Well, so that was it—why they picked me up in the first place. Before I could answer she was running on about going to Rome.

"I know His Holiness is far too busy with the state the world's in today to grant audiences with every Tom, Dick, and Harry, but Father Finney says His Holiness is a lot more concerned with Tom, Dick, and Harry than you would think. I say at least *try*. It would be the experience of a lifetime if an audience is granted."

She went on about a stained-glass window she took in memory of her mother at St. Veronica's in Sylvan Hills, Jesus walking on the water, while we sailed over little pools of water in the road, mirages when you got to them. Mac let her and the car run on, him punching and fussing with the dashboard, half-listening to what she said and half-listening for knocks in the motor. Everything was so automatic you didn't hardly need a driver, driver was just there for looks.

When she wasn't on religion she went back to New Jersey and told which neighbor ladies played bridge and which ones played canasta and how far Sylvan Hills was from Atlantic City and who decorated Early American and who had homemade Swedish card tables from Altman's they didn't have to pay New York tax on, on account of it was New Jersey—while I looked out my rolled-down window at the Pyrenees.

I was getting Mac's trick, getting used to her song and the beat, not paying attention to the stutters and hiccups so much anymore, not even listening to the words. I was seeing row after row of the prettiest, slimmest trees slide by and every once in a while a little mountain town that the road turned through with cafés with tables outside under striped awnings and flowers on people's windowsill and a cat curled up on a stone doorstep and maybe at the edge of town old men playing *pétanque* in berets and so serious where their balls landed they didn't even look up from their tape measure to see our chariot making dust through their hometown—then little one-horse gasoline stands with an old-fashioned hand-pump gas tank outside, then cement road signs saying how many kilometers to Pau and places. After a town you turn off into mountains and trees again.

Mac finally said, "Are you hungry, son?"

We took a picnic out in a field full of poppies and sweet peas fenced off from the cows with barbed wire. Some farmer's wife's wash hung out on bushes and fence posts drying. You had to watch where you stepped for cow turds.

The picnic was mapped out where everything went and who sat where, it was so scientific and sanitary it took longer to set up than to eat. Mrs. Mac took one side of the folding table sitting on a collapsible chair with a pillow with an inner tube in it. Mac sat across from her and me in between. Took a while to get the wax paper and tinfoil off of everything. Eating equipment was the same plastic as in airplanes. They kept their bottled water—Vichy, Perrier, and Vittel—in the portable icebox full of ice, and we drank out of Dixie cups, all the way from Dixie.

I had forgotten how Americans do their food.

But I remembered my manners enough to wipe the chicken grease off my face and look up from dinner and see how the folks were making out. Fine, thank you, but not putting much chow down. We smiled across the table like Emily Post for a minute, then I dug back into my chicken leg.

The McHenrys concentrated more on dried biscuits and a chunk of cheese. She maybe swallowed half a sardine then took about twenty different pills. She had the shakes again and got crumbs scattered all over herself. There was a row of medicine bottles around her paper plate she kept moving around like a game of checkers. Her main dish was red-white-and-blue capsules washed down with a Perrier chaser.

Mac played with a Ry-Krisp cracker and some pimento cheese spread, but he had an ulcer and had to watch what he put in his stomach. He had to wait it out till we got done to go to his after-dinner cigar—a good one, in a metal tube instead of cellophane—and offered me one. I said no thanks but he popped it in my shirt pocket anyway, for later on.

Later we all three of us sat in the car a spell with the car doors open and the flies buzzing in and out, her with her skinny legs crossed and swatting at bugs with a rolled-up Paris *Herald-Tribune.* Then she said to excuse her please, she had to go to the little girl's room. She sat still till Mac climbed out of his side of the car and came around and helped her out of hers. She took her Kleenex and her pocketbook strapped to her shoulder and went off to the woods.

Mac got back behind the wheel and sat sprinkling his cigar into a built-in ashtray. Then he went to playing with the buttons that ran the car windows up and down—you had to watch your elbows when he did that—and looked off to the trees where his wife had went. He turned around to look at me, his eyes as sad as the cocker spaniel eyes on his necktie. Then he came out with it:

"She's the bravest little spirit. Heart of a lion, that little lady." Looked over my shoulder through the back windowpane, then lowered his voice as if she could hear: "Never complains, never mentions a word about it. Parkinson's disease. She's had Parkinson's disease over a year now. Fourteen months. A terrible thing, an awful thing. It just tears a person's nerves to pieces."

I tried to think of something sympathetic to say but all I could get up was the sour taste of my picnic.

"She takes it like a trouper. Would you believe it, that little lady weighed one twenty-five our last anniversary?"

I doubted now she weighed eighty-five pounds soaking wet.

"Up all night, some nights—and the drugs don't seem to take hold anymore. What that little lady has been through—you wouldn't believe the human body could take. It's beyond anything, anything a person can imagine. And never . . ."

He turned back to the dash and I couldn't hear the end of it, it was so mumbled. Played with the pushbutton cigarette lighter, monkeyed with the buttons for the windshield wipers till he got them wiping, looking like long bug feelers, wiping along dry glass. Pushed another button and water squirted out of the hood someplace, like rain pouring upside-down, or tears.

"Oh, we've been to doctors doctors doctors. Specialists, everybody." He named me a list of hospitals and clinics and doctors. "They all say the same thing, not a hope in the world." He gave a sigh out of happiness. "Only a miracle. But she's a fighter—so'm I. With God's help, maybe—just *maybe*. It's in God's hands now. He works in mysterious ways, you know, and his eye, they say, is on the sparrow."

All of a sudden he shut off the waterworks and the wipers and sat up straight in his seat.

"We heard about Lourdes—I guess you have, too. Miracles have happened there, miraculous cures. Every year there's documented proved miracles. Just maybe— with the blessed intervention of St. Bernadette . . ."

I could see his face in the rearview mirror and I quick looked off from his eyes when I saw they were wet. I looked where his wash-and-wear shoulders were sticking up pitiful and cigar smoke curling around his bald place.

Kleenex up to his face wiping his eyes out—no automatic button for that. He asked me to pray for her and I said I would.

They both missed seeing an actual old-time castle rising up out of the valley like out of a storybook, standing on its own private hill to keep the invaders off. Mr. McHenry was too busy trying to find the right turnoff into Lourdes and dodging in and out of the summer traffic—and she missed it, too, talking about which Pope was responsible for making St. Bernadette a genuine saint and all the technicalities of the case. But I twisted around to watch my castle all the way out of sight. That castle was about the last natural satisfying sight I saw, because the next thing I saw was Lourdes.

Every place you looked was a shop window or umbrella booth loaded with the world's worst ten-cent-store holy junk, even the main drag, the whole town one long weary stretch of stupid shit for sale. Place like Lourdes where sick people come from all over to get cured brings out the worst petty grabbiness in the French—they don't miss a trick to make a franc out of somebody's misery.

Here it was—every shape of bottle of holy water and glass caskets of splinters of the cross and Jesus in cheap gilty picture frames strung with fake-pearl rosary beads or Bernadette by the dozens with Mother Mary beside her all aglow with silver-paint tears in her eyes. For kids there was dolls dolled up like nuns or maybe Jesus when he was little, his heart on his stomach shaped like a Valentine.

If Jesus could've been in that Cadillac with us, riding down the streets of Lourdes, he would've stopped the car and got out and took a bullwhip to the whole money-sucking marketplace. But none of it fazed the McHenrys. To them it was just holy typical Woolworth's—no harm to it—but me, I had to shut my eyes not to look anymore.

When I opened up again we were at the church plaza and Mr. McHenry was trying to ease Black Beauty into a shady parking spot next to a rock wall. We got parked and got out. Mrs. McHenry shook herself out a little. She was getting somewhat worked up.

Then she walked nervous over to the edge of the plaza to look and say how magnificent the cathedral was. She was worried whether they'd put color film or black and white in the camera, couldn't remember which. Tested the sunshine with her light meter, took a chance she had color, and took a picture of the church.

Mr. Mac took me aside and said low, whispering, "How are you fixed for money, son?"

I was going to tell him the truth of it, but before I could show him my skimpy money clip he shoved some beautiful color French franc notes into my shirt pocket, next to the cigar he gave me.

Before I could mumble thanks, or touch my hand to the money, he walked away fast to help the Mrs. with her camera.

Then we went into this big open plaza stretched out in front of the church where we came up against the sick people.

Well, I heard of people who came down here for miracles but I never expected to meet them in person. I guess I figured they came at night, on the quiet. But here was a whole world of them, awful sick people, some of them dying, laid out in wheelbarrow beds and sitting up in basket chairs or rolled along, grown people, in big baby carriages. The standing ones held on tight to their crutches and aluminum supporters, with nurses and family propping them up all the way across an acre of cement plaza out in the blazing afternoon sun. It was quiet as a tomb all around. People waited patient in line to get at the holy water, nobody pushing or arguing who's next, just waiting with their rosary beads and prayers and the nurses shooing away flies. It was well regulated, nuns tiptoed through whispering where to go and directing traffic. I hung back with the McHenrys, wondering which way was out.

Me and the McHenrys went down an aisle of wicker chairs with wheels and handles to move them around. The McHenrys looked in on everybody, to show sympathy or just curious, but not me. I stared straight ahead into Mac's wash-and-wear creases not to look at anybody, but I heard them. All down the way I heard them snuffling up nose drops and grinding their teeth and coughing way low in their stomach. I smelled medicine. I felt sick people looking at me, looking right inside me, but I never looked back. Afraid of seeing dead eyes sunk back in their skulls saying to me, "Who're you, strutting through here healthy as a horse and acting Catholic?" Oh, they knew me, the ones in the baskets.

Then I got to lagging behind. The McHenrys moved on up ahead, and a lady with her legs cut off rolled by in a motor chair with an umbrella strapped to her back. Saw where her stubs stuck out from under a blanket and started sweating. She rolled between me and the McHenrys but I took up a trot and passed her, to catch up.

We finally got to the grotto where the miracles happened. Stood around on the edge of the crowd looking into this cave with candles lit back in the rocks and a statue of a lady saint on a ledge with flowers and a halo. Mr. McHenry said it was St. Anne and the Mrs. said it was Mary, take your pick. Arched up over everything from the ground up, covered over about every inch of cave wall, was a bunch of crutches and trusses and old antique girdles and rusty braces with all kind of artificial legs and such parts of people, wood and metal, strung up there for decoration, like a hockshop, left behind after people had miracles and didn't have any more use for them.

Mrs. McHenry got nervous to get so near salvation and it got her Parkinson's worked up again. She trembled her worst yet. He tried to ease her out of it and said *now, now* and took her arm, but she was straining and shaking, pushing ahead of him through the people, trying for front row.

Meanwhile I was doing my best to hang back and get lost. But she took hold of my wrist and dragged me right along with her like her kid. We were getting right up close to the grotto with candles reflected in everybody's eye like fever and you could smell old damp crutch wood moldy from being so long in a cave—when all of a sudden the crowd parted down the middle like the Red Sea. They didn't open up for us, but for something that was crawling along by itself, headed for the cave like us. I shouldn't've looked.

It couldn't walk, it had to crawl. There wasn't no face —it had a black mask on with eyeholes cut out, and I saw the eyes. It was looking at me and it was crawling up by me. I tried to push on up ahead, but there was too much crowd in front of me.

It was wearing a black sweater, all ravelings, and some kind of raggedy dress, little stubs of legs sticking out of the dress with the feet curled up like hands, long curled-up fingers for toes, the feet boxed up in wooden clogs to push along with. Somebody had cut the sweater arms out for flippers to fit through—that's all it had for arms, flippers —or more like chicken wings after your chicken's been plucked and boiled. It kept sliding, crawling, oozing closer, looking up at *me*—I swear to God—out of that black awful mask.

I near fainted. I said to Mac, "I don't feel too good, I got to go."

I don't know if he heard me or not, because he was busy making the sign of the cross in front of Mary or whoever it was. Then the Mrs. let loose of me to make the sign, too, so I just pulled away and took off. I had to step over that thing to get out, but I did, and it never touched me.

I spun by rows and rows of sick people in their baskets without them ever seeing me. Kept my eyes fastened on the plaza gate. That way I never had to look at nobody's sick eyes, and nobody saw mine. I made it. I got out of the gate ready to drop, my chest heaving like a frog's blowers, head dizzy and heart pains, pooped. I got hold of a tree trunk, and held on.

I didn't drop dead or even faint. I held on scraping my face against the side of that tree till I could slide down comfortable and sit back against the tree trunk. The whole time I waited for them I sat that way outside the plaza looking up into the blue. There was some kid's red kite flying high up, way up over the town. I kept turned away like that, turned off cripples and corpses and church and Bernadette and all, watching a kite flying while my sweat dried. I got the sense back in my head and my heartbeat back to normal. I saw myself like a red kite, away up and out of it.

When the McHenrys came back I was all right. I was deep daydreaming in the clouds, almost asleep. I saw them coming along. I jarred myself back awake again and stood up. First thing I noticed, Mac's old lady looked changed. Both of them beamed, and she was way calmed down from before. She was calmed down from her Parkinson's, but excited about something at the same time. Mr. McHenry carried her cameras and her Kleenex, and held her arm for her, too.

She took a big breath with her eyes looking upward, showing the whites, and almost fell over me saying, "I'm well I'm well I'm well, I know I'm well!"

Mr. McHenry nodded, proud.

"I think she is. I think she's cured. I was right beside her when it happened, when the water—"

"Oh, I know! I felt it touch, healing, and St. Bernadette standing right beside me, *her* touch, healing, heavenly, by the grace of God—I *know!*"

She put her hands out in front of her clutched together, praying, and I saw where her hands were out of the shakes, steady as a statue's, like anybody's, like mine.

"Dear blessed Bernadette and Mary Mother of God, we'll come here every day and just *live* here, close to you."

She took on like that, happy, her eyes rolled back in her head sleepy-looking she was so relaxed. Mac was saying something about donating a window until she finally almost slid off his arm—that's how detached she was—so I took her other arm and him and me carried her like a sack of wet wash back to the car.

All the way she kept talking miracle, miracle, miracle and mumbling Hail Marys and thanking the people responsible. She was grateful to St. Bernadette, Mary, Jesus, God, Father Finney, Mr. McHenry, and even me. Generally, I can't work up enough faith to move anthills, but I had to admit that *something* happened down there in that cave to turn off this lady's St. Vitus dance. She strolled along limp as a dishrag, not a shake or a shiver left in her. Just talk and prayers—and I guess I would've talked plenty myself, and maybe prayed, if a miracle ever happened to me.

Then it all fell apart at the car. Right away we saw where somebody had stole the hubcaps off the wheels while we were gone. Mr. McHenry saw it first—he let go of her arm he was so set back. Then she guessed something was wrong and looked and saw what it was. Good thing I still had hold of her. She went all to pieces as soon as she saw what was done to the car. The shakes thundered through her all over again.

She busted out crying, hysterical. Mac tried to soft-soothe her down out of it, but he was plenty rattled his-self to see his hubcaps missing. He told her it was going to be all right, but she didn't believe him. She pulled loose from me, shaking terrible, and went all the way around that car, twice, kneeled down on her knees at every single wheel where a hubcap used to be. She never paid any attention to how her skirt was up. She was just wild with crying and grief.

Her face got so twisted up it was awful to look at. The sunglasses dangled down from just one ear, tears so wet on her face they were drooping off her chin. Finally she couldn't see for the tears and had to feel of the wheel bolts with her hands, blind, testing to satisfy herself it was true. It was true all right. It was probably done with a screwdriver—easiest thing in the world—I've seen kids do it.

Mr. McHenry stood behind her with his hand on her shoulder saying *now, now,* but his own face was strained unhappy too. Looked like he was thinking, how could it happen to *me?*—why would anybody do that way to *my* automobile? He was all the sad Americans that ever got to France and got took, ever got pickpocketed anyplace, little boy beat, surprised at the world, hole in his pocket where his marbles leaked through, numb after his kite string broke wondering what happened.

Miracle was over. It got too sticky for me. I couldn't look at her anymore, the way she was, or him either. Didn't know how to back off graceful—it's not as easy to pry loose from people as to pry hubcaps off.

"I guess I'll take my gear along, go to a little hotel I saw down the way."

Couldn't look him in the eye when I said it. I looked at the sad-eye cocker spaniels painted on his necktie.

He mumbled something—yes, sure—and unlocked for

me. I took my guitar out and my duffel and said so long. Him and me shook hands, but she was too collapsed and shaky to. He went to her with a wad of Kleenex, and that's the way I left them.

Walked around till dark—the darker it got, the better. That way I didn't have to see no more city of Lourdes. I ended up in the ramshackle section where I felt at home, wrong side of the tracks where I belonged.

There was a little pinch-face kid carrying a goldfish in a cellophane bag of water, and I asked him where the girls hang out. He told me where and I gave him a couple of francs to buy another goldfish with.

Next thing I knew I was knocking on a door that came open to music, a big room with low lights. Old-time player piano in the corner, playing "Auprès de Ma Blonde," switched to "When the Saints Go Marching In" soon as I marched in. Deep green drapes like underwater, soft divans with silky pillows. I was the only customer in sight. Girls came on in their working clothes, a dozen of them. Japanese bathrobes thin as tissue paper. Tucked my St. Chris out of sight and lit Mac's cigar. Ring-around with butterflies, alive-o.

The Late Miss America

THE OUTSIDE of her sunglasses reflected like mirrors, so that if the fellow smiling that funny smile tried to look and searched for her eyes, he would only see twin images of himself looking back. But he did not look. Instead, she caught herself staring at him. It was a good thing the sunglasses hid her eyes—she was used to being stared at herself (that was what show business was, Sid always said)—but Sid had taught her how not to stare back. You never stared back, or the person that was looking at you might get ideas. The fellow on the next balcony did not look the type that got ideas, but you never knew. Why did he just keep sitting there like that, staring at the ocean instead of in her direction, and not even trying to get a tan? He was there yesterday, too, and the day before. What was he smiling at if he wasn't smiling at her?

She never smoked unless she was with Sid, in some theater manager's office, or at some booking agency. Mom sent her all the articles from newspapers and *Reader's Digest* about cancer from cigarettes, so she was careful never to inhale. She only smoked to look older than nineteen. Now, she fumbled for the package of cigarettes in the pocket of her terry-cloth robe, then put the robe over her shoulders (the feeling reminded her, all of a sudden, of the ermine cape Mr. Nichols put around her on WBXG-TV, in Omaha, when he crowned her Miss Nebraska) and walked over to the low dividing wall between balconies.

"Excuse me. Do you happen to have a light?"

His head jerked up from wherever he had been looking —when he turned to her his face was white, the smile had disappeared.

She caught her breath and touched the place where her heartbeat quickened, "Is that a gun?"

There was a pistol lying in his lap, and even as he tried to cover it with his hands he must have known she had seen what it was.

"What?" He opened his hands and looked at the pistol like a little boy caught doing something dumb. "It's a souvenir, it's not loaded."

"I was just asking for a light. I didn't mean to bother you. I didn't know you had a gun."

"I didn't know anybody was there."

She stood there practicing stage presence—a little nervous about seeing the pistol: but it was funny-looking and didn't look real like the ones on TV—holding the prop cigarette, unlit, between them. He finally noticed the cigarette. He did not even search his pockets before saying, "A light? No. I'm sorry."

"That's OK," she said quickly, but her reassurance did nothing to alter the hurt look on his face. "That's OK. I've got a lighter here someplace."

A gold cigarette lighter was part of the bounty that came with winning the Miss Nebraska title—along with a lot of other things she never used that Mom was keeping for her back in Lincoln. She turned to fumble through a collection of bottles (nail polish, Coca-Cola, Sunshower lotion) scattered across a beach towel—plus half of a pastrami sandwich, plastic hair curlers, and a movie magazine with "The Curse of Patty Duke" on the cover. She found the gold lighter in the pages of the magazine.

"See?" She held the lighter out to him.

He got up, almost painfully, and came over to the dividing wall, holding the pistol downward. He took the cigarette lighter somewhat shakily and flicked it on. She loved the way men usually cupped a flame with their hands, and you dipped your face into the bowl of their hands when they lit your cigarette—but he did not cup the lighter flame, because of the pistol in his other hand.

She offered him a cigarette, but he shook his head no.

"I noticed you before," she said. "I mean, I noticed how you never get any sun. You allergic? The sun's terrific down here. I'm getting a fabulous tan."

She drew apart the wings of her robe the way you did at Atlantic City, and looked down at herself. All she was wearing, besides sunglasses, was a Princess Prim bikini that she wore only for getting a tan. The fellow from the next balcony looked down when she did—he was a man, after all—and nodded yes. Then he gave her back her lighter.

"How come you carry a gun around?"

She wondered what Mom would say if she knew her daughter was having a conversation with a fellow with a gun in his hand.

"It's a kind of an antique." He looked shyly at the pistol. "You couldn't do any real damage with it, it's got no range. It's what they consider a lady's-type pistol. I got it off a guy in Key West. I don't think you can even get shells for one of these things anymore."

He spun the oversize cylinder to show her the cartridge chambers were empty. When she saw the pistol was harmless, she lost interest in it and wanted to talk about herself, and why she was down in Florida—but with men you always talked about things that interested them first.

"If it doesn't work, what do you carry it around for then?"

"It works if you can get shells for it. I've got a collection—not pistols, rifles."

"Antique ones?"

"No, real."

"Are you going to shoot somebody?"

She smiled her prize-winning smile at him to show she was only kidding, but his smile faded.

"Not with this thing."

That seemed about as far as the subject of firearms could be stretched—but with a man, you kept talking about him until he got interested in you.

"Are you a soldier, by any chance?"

"Why?" He looked hard at her, his eyes half-closed. She did not like his look when he did that. His eyes were nice, and a nice color—they were his best feature, actually —so he was better off to keep them open.

"I just wondered. It's your shirt you wear. It looks like an army shirt."

"Yeah, it is. It's my only one, so I have to wear it. I was in, but I'm out now. On what they call a Section Eight."

"What's a Section Eight?"

"It's just a discharge." He watched her face a moment, then added, "It's a medical."

"Oh," she said. "Are you down here for your health?"

"No," he said. "I'm waiting for the convention to start."

"No kidding? So am I. That's what I'm down here for. I'm in show business. My manager is in Miami Beach right this minute getting me booked into a terrific show-case for the convention. I do impressions of famous people. Vocalists, movie stars—you know, well-known celebrities and all. Sid says 'impressions' sounds higher-class than 'impersonations.' He says if you're a girl and you go around saying you do impersonations it leaves you wide open to get called a female impersonator."

She smiled her special on-camera smile waiting for him to laugh at the punch line, but he didn't laugh. All he said was, "Who's Sid?"

"Oh, Sid. He's my manager. Agent, actually. I create all my own routines myself, Sid just gets me my bookings. How I got started was last year I was runner-up in the Miss America pageant. I was Miss Nebraska."

She waited for him to say something. A little time passed before he finally said, "Congratulations."

"Oh, that was last year. And I didn't win, I was only runner-up. But Sid always calls me Miss America anyway, and gets me billed as Miss America. 'Who knows the dif-ference,' Sid always says. One time Sid told a theater manager he represented Miss America and the theater manager said, 'Since when did you sign up Miss America?' and Sid said, 'Since last year. She was Miss America last year,' and the theater manager said, 'You mean you're handling the late Miss America?' and Sid said, 'Not late. Ex. Late means dead,' and the theater manager said, 'Same difference. Anybody that was Miss America last year, this year they're dead.' "

She waited for the fellow on the next balcony to laugh or something. It was funny the way he never laughed.

"Anyway," she went on, "I got Sid in a package deal with the Low Notes. I mean Sid got me. The Low Notes are these vocalists. They're colored. They were supposed to go on tour with us and we got as far as Jacksonville and they found out the segregation was de facto and they would have to stay at a different hotel from Sid and me unless they went to court so they said nothing doing, and broke their contract. Sid blew his stack. We were a package deal, and the Florida bookings were for both of us. Sid said that was the last time they'd walk out on a contract in the USA and Lawrence, their baritone, said, 'You mean we're going to be *black*listed?'—so what could Sid say?"

She couldn't tell if the fellow on the next balcony was paying attention or not. He was looking out at the ocean again.

"I don't care what the Low Notes say, I really love it down here. Down here the sun is the greatest. So far I never used my balcony awning, not even once. But I noticed how you keep yours rolled down all the time. All you get is shade that way."

He opened his eyes all the way and looked at the awning for the first time. "I guess I didn't think of it."

"You're a riot," she said. "My gosh, how can you miss all that fabulous sun all day?" She showed him the awning crank on his side of the balcony, and he stiffly turned the handle to roll back the candy-striped canvas. "It won't kill you, for crying out loud." His face was ghostly as he squinted into the sudden flood of sun. "Sunshine contains vitamin C, just like orange juice. I mean, if you're sick, that's what Florida is *for*."

"I'm not sick," he said, and she did not like the way he looked at her when he said it.

But she was used to being looked at in all kinds of ways, and if he wanted to look at her with his eyes half-closed it was all right with her. She sat sidesaddle on the low dividing wall, and if he happened to look down on her side of the balcony he would see the splendid stems of her legs sprouting out of the terry cloth. But he did not look down.

"It's funny, the day you win. When I won Miss Nebraska, I mean. I cried I was so happy. I felt like from then on I would just go around being a winner all my life. You know that feeling?"

"No," he said.

"I mean, I really thought I would go on and win Miss America in Atlantic City and all. Actually I almost *was* Miss America. I was runner-up. In fact, I got more points in the talent category than Miss America got. And the other girls voted me Miss Congeniality for being the nicest. None of the other girls could stand the girl that won Miss America. She was sort of stuck-up, and she didn't know the first thing about projection. You should have seen her project. But when she won Miss America you had to be a good sport about it. I was a good sport about it when I was on-camera, but I cried in the ladies' room. What finally cheered me up was knowing I was at least Miss Congeniality and the most talented and all. Mr. Nichols on WBXG-TV said I had talent right down to my toenails."

She stretched out one leg, arching her foot until the toes spread apart like a tiny jeweled fan. The fellow on the next balcony looked at her toes, then looked away again. She could tell he was not the type that got ideas. Anyway, as long as you stayed on your side of the balcony what could the other person think?

"The Omaha Jaycees voted me this scholarship to go to college on, but I backed out. I met Sid right after I was runner-up in Atlantic City and Sid picked up my contract in this package deal with the Low Notes and the next thing I knew I was in show business. Just like that."

"And that's how you got to be Miss America?"

"Miss Ne*braska*. Sid calls me Miss America, but in Atlantic City I was really only a runner-up."

"Maybe I'll get to be a big name someday, too." He was smiling that funny smile again, so she couldn't tell if he was being sarcastic or not.

"I didn't say I was a big name. I just started in show business, for crying out loud. It's not easy. Sid says it's a rat race, basically. You're not in show business by any chance, are you?"

"No."

"It's hard to be a big name unless you're in show business."

"Do you read the newspapers?" asked the fellow on the next balcony.

She shook her head no. "I read *Variety*. Sometimes I read *Show Business* when Sid's finished with it. I'm not much of a reader. I tried to read Zsa Zsa Gabor's autobiography, but I couldn't get into it."

"Start reading the newspapers. Down at the convention, when you get there. You might see my name in the papers."

"No kidding?" She couldn't tell if he was kidding or not, with that smile. "Maybe we'll both be big names." On second thought, he looked too young to be a politician, so how could he be a big name at the convention? "I don't know if you believe in dreams or not, but just the other night I dreamed the President showed up at the nightclub Sid booked me into, and caught my act."

Something about the way the fellow's eyes were open now made her think he believed in dreams too.

"Say," she said, "you want to see something?"

He hesitated a moment before saying, "OK. Sure."

She pulled up the collar of her terry-cloth robe, sucked in her cheeks, and did Katharine Hepburn.

"That was Katharine Hepburn," she said.

He held the pistol in his armpit while he applauded. Then he crossed his arms and stood watching her, the pistol in one hand dangling down below his crossed arms.

She opened her eyes wide, pursed her lips, and let the robe fall. She supported her right elbow with her left hand and punctuated the air with her cigarette. Bette Davis.

"You're good," he said, applauding again. "I recognized her."

"Didn't I tell you I was talented? I do men, too."

Maybe he did get ideas after all, because his smile became a grin, and when she looked down at herself she had to smile back.

"For crying out loud, *that* doesn't make any difference. It's all gestures, and how you project."

She was going to do James Cagney singing "Yankee Doodle Dandy," to prove she could do men too, when the telephone rang. At first the sound seemed to hurt the fellow on the next balcony in his stomach—he held the pistol there with both hands. They listened together for the second ring, and then he said calmly, the pistol dangling at his side, "I think it's your phone."

"Mine? Yipes, it must be Sid!"

She dashed away, the empty arms of her robe flapping after her as she slammed through the French doors and into the room. She flung herself across the bed and jerked the telephone receiver from its stand.

"Sid? It's me. Is that you?"

"No, ma'am." It was the motel manager. "I was just going to send the housemaid up to shut your windows, there's a storm coming up."

"Oh," she said. "That's OK. I'm here. I'll shut them.

Listen, you didn't by any chance get a telephone call for me, did you?"

"No, ma'am, no calls."

A cold wind blew across her face as she stepped through the French doors, and she felt the first heavy drops of rain. An ugly sweep of clouds was building up over the Atlantic. The blue-green of the water had drained away to gray—a beachboy was running along the oceanfront gathering towels out of the sand.

Somehow, even in the rain, she had expected to find the fellow on the next balcony still standing there, with the pistol in his hand. But he was gone. The French doors to his room had blown open, and she saw a pair of shoes lying beside a wrought-iron table. It was raining in his shoes.

"Yoo-hoo! Hey, it's me!"

There was no answer. She leaned as far as she dared across the wall between balconies. The heavy rain swept in windblown from the sea, and she felt water trickling down the back of her neck. She rescued her bottle of Sunshower lotion and a net bag of pink curlers before ducking inside. She shut the French doors after her, and turned down the glass jalousie slats to keep the rain from blowing into the room. It was suddenly dark, and she felt shut into a box.

She switched on all of the lights, even the bed lamps and the fluorescent light in the bathroom. She turned the air-conditioning dial to OFF, but she still felt chilled.

In a couple of days Sid would probably have her contract all ironed out and a fabulous showcase set up. Miami Beach would be crawling with politicians, Sid said, and every night spot on the Beach would be booked solid. The delegates and everybody would be desperate for a little live entertainment after all those dull speeches on the convention floor. Signing Miss America up in a setup like Miami Beach was a cinch, Sid said. Only she wasn't actually Miss America. And that was two weeks ago. She wished Sid would call. She hadn't heard a word from Sid since he left two weeks ago and said to sit tight.

She wished she could talk to somebody. She wished she were back having a conversation with the fellow on the next balcony. Maybe she would write a letter to Mom, but writing a letter wasn't the same as talking to somebody.

Sid said to keep rehearsing, so she started to rehearse Judy Garland in front of the full-length mirror in the bathroom. She would rehearse Judy Garland until it stopped raining. Maybe she would call up the manager of the motel and ask him to connect her to the fellow with the room next to hers and tell him his shoes were getting wet outside in the rain. But that was a dumb thing to do —what kind of ideas would the manager get? She didn't even know the name of the fellow in the next room.

Maybe she should have crossed over to his balcony and picked up his shoes out of the rain. No, she shouldn't have. She was glad she didn't cross over. Once you cross over to another person's balcony, that's when they start getting ideas.

She would go on practicing Judy Garland until it stopped raining. Judy Garland was her favorite impression, and it gave her a chance to vocalize. So she began singing "Over the Rainbow" in the bathroom, watching herself in the mirror—but she couldn't get it right somehow, she couldn't concentrate. She wondered if the fellow next door could hear her singing "Over the Rainbow"? She kept trying, and then got as far as "bluebirds fly" and couldn't seem to go on, she couldn't get it right. She kept feeling cold and wanting somebody to talk to, and she couldn't keep from remembering about the shoes on the next balcony filling up with rainwater.

Keepers

T H E Y S A Y the new mayor pulled strings to get Elberta
Sims into the state hospital down at Milledgeville, where
they are keeping her. Otherwise she would've had to have
been bound over by the grand jury. The way she told it at
the inquest was that her daddy took over five years to die
of his stroke, and now her momma was pulling the same
stunt.

At least her daddy lingered peaceful enough, but not
her momma. If you forgot and left her cane or a broom-
stick anywheres near the bed she would take and hit you
with it with her one good arm, the one that wasn't par-
alyzed. Poor Elberta. She never could get married. And
now never would, it looked like.

The telephone company put a telephone in. It was an added expense. But living alone with a sick old woman, how else could Elberta get in touch with the doctor? Also, she could call up and get groceries delivered. The grocery man came out in a car and brought the mail too. The mail was nothing, only circulars and *Life* magazine. Elberta had not stepped foot in town in three years, at least.

When the telephone rang she thought it was the doctor saying he would put a prescription in with the drugstore, but it was not. It was some fellow.

"How do you do, Miss Sims. My name is A. M. Oliver, some call me 'Prince.' "

"Fine, thank you."

"The reason I called you up is to solicit your vote."

"What did you say your name was?"

"Oliver. I'm running for mayor of Watershed."

"Whatever became of the other mayor? Did he die?"

"Frankly, Miss Sims, the Democratic Party thinks Mayor Childs has been mayor for a good long term now, and is getting forgetful of his constituents in his declining years. They gave the nomination to yours truly."

"To who?"

"To me. A. M. Oliver. Some call me 'Prince.' My daddy was assistant manager of the Tri-State Cannery for years and years, and I followed in his footsteps until drafted. I went to Young Harris College by working my way through. Then served in the Korean War with a Good Conduct medal. I read law with Colonel Kincaid after my Honorable Discharge and have been in politics ever since."

"I thought Colonel Kincaid died."

"No indeed. He's retired, but he's not dead."

"Are you from around here?"

"I was born here. I went to school in Watershed with

high marks. I have a college degree from Young Harris College."

"I guess the reason I never knew you was I had to go to the county school, out at Gravelly Gap. I had to walk. They wouldn't send the school bus out here and get me."

"That's a shame. That's one of the things the new administration wants to fix. Frankly, Miss Sims, I'm out to solicit your vote in the upcoming election."

"When is it upcoming?"

"In November. And you have to be a registered voter to vote."

"I'm sorry. I am not a voter. And never was."

"Well, here is your chance to be one."

"What did you say your name was?"

"A. M. 'Prince' Oliver. You don't know me, but I am acquainted with you. I looked you up in the telephone book. I also checked on you in the County Clerk's office. According to the records you are a perfectly qualified voter, except for being registered. Now I understand you live way out and too far to come into town easy. But I am volunteering to send a taxicab out to get you. And bring you right up to the courthouse door."

"That is right nice of you, but my momma is down with a stroke. I keep her night and day."

"You are surely dedicated."

"You never know from one minute to the next whether she will need the bedpan or not."

"That is what I call dedication. They tell me you kept your daddy, before he died, the same way. There is just not that much dedication going around anymore. This day and age. I would say offhand that you and me are birds of a feather. I myself am dedicated to the public service, and that's why I'm running for mayor. You know, we're all keepers of each other, in one way or another. It's even in the Bible."

"Yes sir. You will find it in Genesis. 'Am I my brother's keeper?' "

"I tell you what, Miss Sims. I'm perfectly willing to send somebody out in the same taxi that can stay and keep your momma while you are away. To relieve you at the bedside while you get registered."

"I don't know. I don't trust every Tom, Dick, and Harry anymore. Not since the hosiery mill was put in. There's a new element around town I don't recognize anymore."

"All right. I'll go one better. I'll personally come out in a cab myself. I myself will volunteer to keep your momma for you."

"What did you say your name was?"

"A. M. Oliver. Some call me 'Prince.' "

"Amen?"

"A.*M*. Like A.M. in the morning. Which suits me to a T, for I am an early bird. That will be our campaign slogan: 'A.M. will work for you from A.M. to P.M.' "

"That's a good motto. I hope you win."

"Can I count on your vote?"

"I don't know."

"You just hang on out there. I'm coming out directly in a taxicab. At my own personal expense."

After she hung up she went out in the porch swing and read a *Life* magazine for a while, and waited. Sure enough, he finally came. He was a bigger fellow than he sounded on the telephone. He was good-looking except for getting a little bit bald-headed in the front. He had a necktie on and his sleeves rolled up. Rolled-up sleeves was always a good sign in a man.

"Miss Sims, how do you do?"

"Fine, thank you."

"Didn't I tell you I would be right out in a taxicab?"

"You surely did."

"I'm a man of my word, and that's exactly the kind of dedication I intend to give the taxpayers as your mayor."

"I sure hope you win. And I thank you kindly for coming out."

"Show me where you keep your momma and I'll personally watch over her bedside."

"She's asleep. Watch out, for she is mean. She will strike you with her cane if she gets half a chance."

"I reckon this has been a sore trial for a young girl like you."

"I'm thirty-three years of age. And not getting any younger."

She got in with the taxi man. Driving into town she asked the taxi man if A. M. Oliver was married or not. He said not that he knew of.

It was court week, and the courthouse was naturally crowded. It took Elberta some little time to locate the County Clerk and get registered. Then the clerk gave her a card she could vote with. There was a trial on, and a number of country people were milling about. It was hot in the courthouse. Elberta bought an ice cream on a stick from a colored man with sunglasses on. It was chocolate on the outside and vanilla on the inside, and just hit the spot.

She asked the colored man what the trial was all about and he said he didn't know. It was over some white people.

Elberta went in the courtroom and sat on one of the back benches away from the tobacco spitters, not to get her good shoes dirty. The jury was drinking Coca-Cola. A heavy-set girl from a settlement called Cuthbert was seated on the witness stand. The defendants were three town boys, two of them good-looking. The girl claimed they raped her. Their lawyers said they didn't.

One of the boys was smoking a cigarette. Elberta was surprised the court allowed it. He was not one of the good-looking ones. She wondered if the boys were that new element that works out at the hosiery mill. The girl from Cuthbert said she lived alone with her granddaddy in a little cabin out there. Her granddaddy was blind and never saw what went on. What was a girl doing living out in Cuthbert alone like that in the first place? Well, Elberta was in the same boat herself.

The fat girl was surely not what you would call pretty. Not by a long sight. Elberta could not make up her mind whether the girl was telling a tale or not. She looked like the type that would tell you anything. Elberta just could not believe that the good-looking boys would rape a thing like that. Unless it was the one that smoked. It gave her a funny feeling in her insides to think of somebody raping some helpless girl out in the country like that.

But she couldn't stay and see how the trial turned out on account of the taxi man waiting. She got back in the taxi and went home.

A. M. Oliver was sitting on the porch steps reading a *Life* magazine.

"There's an interesting article in there," Elberta informed him. "On a missionary that got eat up by deadly fish in Rio de Janeiro."

"I read that one," said he. The taxi man was waiting, so he had to get going.

"I sure hope you get elected."

"Frankly, I think the good people of Watershed are ready for a change."

"I reckon some of them are. I know I am."

"Just remember: 'A.M. will work for you from A.M. to P.M.' "

"I think that's the smartest motto I ever heard. I believe it will get you elected."

A. M. Oliver put on the nicest smile.

"Tell me something, Miss Sims. Do you like chocolate ice-cream sodas?"

"I surely do."

"All right, the very next time you get to town I'm going to buy you the biggest chocolate ice-cream soda in the drugstore. And that's a promise."

"I am much obliged."

"It's I'm the one that's obliged to you."

After he drove off, Elberta went upstairs to see how her momma was. Well, A. M. Oliver might make a dandy mayor, but he was not great shakes at nursing care. Her momma had got loose from the belt Elberta tied her arm to the bedstead with, and rolled out of bed with her bed covers and all. There she was in the middle of the floor, where she had dirtied herself something awful. She had not only dirtied herself but she had dirtied her bed covers and the rug and everything. Elberta felt like crying. Cleaning it all up, she finally did cry. After such a nice day. She got her momma back in bed with clean sheets and a fresh nightgown. She forgot the belt was lying there, and her momma took and hit Elberta across the face with it.

At first Elberta cried some more, then she got so nervous she couldn't see straight. After such a nice day. She went and got the pillow off the floor and put it over her momma's head. Then she sat on it. In a little while her momma stopped wiggling under the pillow.

Elberta went straight out of the house and walked all the way into town in her good shoes. The courthouse was letting out, and there were automobiles all over. Elberta went into the drugstore and took a stool with an empty one next to it. She sat and sat there. When the waitress asked her two or three times what'll it be, she wasn't saying.

The Song of the
Hourglass Salesman

Dear Lloyd (*wherever you may be*),

Fate is funny, Son. A month or so ago your old Dad—
80 in '80: "Warren came in with the century," my precious mother, and your own beloved grandmother
(*though you never met her*), used to say—believe it or
not had to sleep sitting up in the Greyhound bus terminal
in Jacksonville, Florida. Before that, the Imperial Rooms
at one dollar per night in Atlanta. There was nothing
imperial about them: you stood in line to use the bathroom. I will not go into the subject of vermin, or a
wino in the next cubicle with delirium tremens. A so-
called mattress cover is included in the dollar, but if it
ever saw the inside of a washtub I will eat my hat.

Never say die, as they say. Not many moons ago a maiden lady in Citrus, Florida, in a wheelchair, suffering dropsy and assorted ailments, took me on as aide-de-camp and I did have a roof over my head—albeit a leaky one— for the nonce. A Christian woman in every sense of the word. Bless her heart, she was an animal lover and meant well (I have a way with women of her type, always did) —but I am allergic to cats and dogs.

Well, picture me today in a $75,000 (at least) House & Garden *home, with the genteel hostess of the manse (in her seventies, I suspect—but she is not saying) at my beck and call. She is right this minute out at Park 'n Market to purchase a six-pack of Seminole beer due to a casual remark I made about what I saw in a Coca-Cola bottling plant once. She is a Coca-Cola drinker. I cannot stand so-called soft drinks in any shape or form. As soon as she went out I took the trouble to take inventory of her silverware. Every piece is a first-rate original, each item deftly inscribed with a fancy "G" (for Greenleaf), from pickle fork to soup tureen. Think of it—she has been out nearly an hour, buying beverages and what-not, leaving a perfect stranger alone on the premises! I could have been a crook for all she knew, with a truck parked around the corner.*

The refined atmosphere appealed to my nature the moment I was carried inside. (Yes, your old Dad was on the horizontal for a change, having passed out on Mrs. Greenleaf's lawn.) Don't worry, Son—nothing serious. Due to skipping lunch, after a skimpy breakfast. Also, had removed my hat in the heat of midday (forgetting I was in Florida!) when addressing a police officer who inquired about my sample case (full of egg timers I am promoting, minature three-minute hourglasses, a unique item if there ever was one—but Sunshine City is a private development of suburban homes for Senior Citizens, and

133

people today—even the Seniors—do not realize how much more digestible a soft-boiled egg is than fried, with a No Salesmen sign at the gate), and was felled by a mild sunstroke. Mrs. G immediately adjusted the air conditioning to suit my personal comfort. She apologized for the newspapers scattered about, having just mopped the floor and put papers down to walk on, but as far as I am concerned (and I told her so) the place is as neat as a pin. (After that flophouse, and Miss Dowd's ramshackle abode, you bet!) Clean ashtrays galore—though I do not smoke, never have and never will—and waste baskets (empty, all) all over the place.

Here is a mystery that has puzzled me all my life: how does a gracious lady like Mrs. G see fit to invite an oldster like me she doesn't know from Adam into her high-class picturesque home like a long-lost brother—or a husband, missing for years (a victim of kidnapping or amnesia) who turns up without warning on the door-step? A war hero or a winning politician could not have been made to feel more welcome. With no questions asked. I do not know whether it is my personality or salesmanship or what.

The more I think about it, the more at home I feel. Frankly, I cannot help but be struck—as I glance around this cozy nest—that it could be made into a perfect "sailor's snug harbor," so to speak. I know I could ease in here, get next to Mrs. G, and be set for life. When in my age bracket you begin to think about these things. Like an old dog chasing its tail, I seem to be traveling in circles of late. The siren song of the open road is naturally music to your ears at your age (I was the same myself when younger), but I have reached the point, you might say, of no return.

I am sorry I ever signed those papers for you to enlist. And could have kicked myself for doing so.

Stepping on Mrs. G's homemade hooked rugs (hooking rugs is a hobby of hers) is like stepping back into Martha Washington's day (though dangerous as the devil underfoot). The spinning wheel in one corner is the real McCoy and worth three hundred dollars if it's worth a dime—not counting the patriotic lampshade it is fitted with: a parchment facsimile of the Declaration of Independence. You just do not go into antiques without money to burn. I love an old-fashioned fireplace, and hers is a dandy—but with an air-conditioner in it, this being Florida. An antique chime clock chimes soothingly every hour on the hour, on the mantelpiece, reminding one and all that time *is running out.*

Yes, Son, tempus fugit—*and there is a lesson there for you, Lloyd. Live each day as if it is your last on earth, for we know not if we shall pass this way again. Also, it is never too late to turn over a new leaf. "Strait is the gate," your precious grandmother used to quote, but I myself was always inclined to take the wayward and meandering path. Guilty, I admit, of more than one "misdemeanor" over the years. Sad but true, I operated somewhat sub rosa all my life.*

(Money, darn it, has always been my weak point. I was never strictly on the up and up where cash was concerned. And will go to my grave regretting it.)

Something in my nature led me astray at an early age. I hope and pray you do not follow in your old Dad's footsteps in this respect! I fell in with a worldly-wise crowd when young and have spent a lifetime trying to undo the damage. Choose your chums with care! Try to associate with the officer class instead of your ordinary (or "ablebodied" as the navy calls them) seamen. As for female companionship, there is penicillin now, I know, but you could be allergic, like me.

(The minute Mrs. G gets back from Park 'n Market I

*am going to ask her point blank who her interior dec-
orator is, though I know darned well she is her own. I am
going to tell her whoever her interior decorator is, he is
tops. Then watch her face.)*

*Lloyd, remember one thing. When you are eventually
discharged (honorably, I hope and pray) from the naval
service of your country, I promise and assure you that you
have a home waiting here, with your old Dad*—no questions asked. *If your discharge should turn out to be other
than honorable, well, I myself would have to plead* mea
culpa (*my own fault, as the Romans used to say*) *to a
dishonorable deed or two in my day. Believe me, I know
from personal experience how easy it is to take a* faux pas
(*French for false step*) *in this world.*

*I actually passed out on Mrs. Greenleaf's lawn this
P.M. and came within an inch of fracturing my skull on
her birdbath. My pulse has not been the same since. She
was instantly at my side like a latter-day Florence Night-
ingale (I told her so) and offered me aspirin, or a doctor,
but I said, "Place an aspirin on a piece of raw meat and
see what happens." My precious mother, your beloved
grandmother, avoided aspirin like the plague. As for a
doctor, I had already diagnosed my own case as skipping
lunch after a skimpy breakfast and removing my hat in
the hot sun. Remember, if I had actually "turned in my
chips" from a coronary occlusion—which is common at
this stage of the game, at my age—well, Son, it would
be too late to let bygones be bygones ever again. There is
no time like the present to forgive and forget the festering
wounds of yesteryear.*

*On the subject of desertion (which is what the divorce
courts call it), as a matter of fact your mother was the
one who deserted me, for another man, though I was "on
the road" at the time and heard it via the grapevine so*

could never verify the fact. Not that I have a single slighting word to say against your stepfather, whoever he is— or fathers, as the case may be. Your mother was my third or fourth "helpmeet" (as the Bible calls them) and only twenty or so years of age (while I was three times that) and ours but a common-law arrangement to begin with, so you can imagine what a shaky start the romance got off to. Well, all that is water under the bridge. Yet, idle regrets do manage to muddy the waters from time to time. You were only four and one-half years old when I last glimpsed you (in a sailor suit, too, like the genuine article you are wearing today) and bright as could be (you uttered your first full-length sentence at eight months), with a teddy bear in hand. More water has flowed under the bridge than I can describe in this letter but let's just say you are looking at a slowed-down old bird on the wing seeking one last nest for the night. I definitely intend to turn over a new leaf (a green one, at that!) and I hope and pray you will see fit to turn one over too. Mrs. G may not know it yet, but she found a soul mate when she found me lying on her front lawn.

What I am getting at is, Lloyd, you have not answered a single one of my many letters to Great Lakes yet. Be that as it may, my intention is to bridge the empty years with heartfelt letters betwixt father and son, and if I can ignite a spark of affection on your part, so be it. Even as I ease into this comfy niche with my well-to-do widowed hostess, there is a prayer on my lips for a future family reunion (minus your mother).

Fate is funny, Son. An atom bomb in the hands of some insane politician (and they are all insane, if you ask me) could wipe us off the face of the earth—you, me, Mrs. G's House & Garden *home included—if the wrong button was pushed . . .*

*   *   *

137

"You're as old as you feel, is the way I look at it."

"So do I, but I realize now where we went wrong. His mother was too young for me, though pretty as a picture in every way. With thin ankles and nice skin—which is my weak spot when it comes to women. Be that as it may, my overriding regret is being kept incommunicado from my boy all these years."

"The generation gap today is a crime."

"Mostly my fault, and his mother's. *Mea culpa,* I admit. I doubt if he ever saw a single one of the many letters I wrote him care of his mother. She wrote me asking me to sign papers for Lloyd to enlist and I could have kicked myself for doing so, without a word from Lloyd on the subject. That was when I began to correspond with him, just before he went into the navy. A one-way correspondence, if there ever was one. For all I know, Lloyd is out on the high seas today. If his ship should be sinking right this minute, I would be the last to know."

"We were childless from the beginning. That was a cross I had to bear. I never knew whether it was on Mr. Greenleaf's side or mine."

"I hate to say a single slighting word against Coca-Cola, since you are so fond of it, but Coke and cigarettes may be at the bottom of it."

"The last time I gave up cigarettes I put on so much weight I just about broke the bathroom scales."

"I don't believe that for one minute. And I hope you don't think I'm being too forward too soon when I admit the first thing I spied when I came to on your lawn this afternoon was the prettiest pair of ankles since Lloyd's mother's the day we walked down the aisle."

"You should have seen them a week after I stopped smoking."

"I don't believe that for one minute. What beats me is

why some handsome beau hasn't waltzed in here yet and swept you right off your feet."

"I'll tell you one reason. I am not the type to lower myself to try and make the acquaintance of some spoiled widower with twenty other women hanging on his neck, that's why!"

"I don't blame you. You are right about the twenty-to-one statistics, too—cholesterol being the major cause of it. Just about the time you ladies are coming into your prime, we spouses have already bowed out with a heart attack. Business pressures, and a fatty diet. Women have a lower center of gravity and are inclined to recline more. My precious mother reclined in a hammock for hours at a stretch, and lived to be four-score and ten—with a heart murmur you could hear all the way across the room."

"I am just going to take the bull by the horns and inquire where you are staying the night."

"As a matter of fact I was all set to take the same bus back to Citrus, the bus I came in on. It passes Lake Seminole, and I am dying to see those cypresses along the shoreline at sundown. In Citrus I am bound to find an old-fashioned guest house of the type I delight in, with a wide veranda and rocking chairs, and a strict landlady to keep the riffraff out."

"As for your bus, the last bus left from Golden Years Plaza at least an hour ago. You don't have a car?"

"I have had dozens in my day. I drove a Packard for years, and a Hudson after that. Did you ever hear of the Detroit Electric before they went out of business? Well, I drove one. I love a fancy automobile and am a skilled driver, if I do say so myself."

"Even if you could get back to Citrus this evening, I doubt if you would find a guest house of any description. They are all motels now, or Hiltons. Anyway, without a car, the only transportation out of Sunshine City after dark is our twenty-four-hour ambulance service, and I surely hope my dinner didn't put you in need of an ambulance!"

"I don't want to sound pushy, but that fancy davenport of yours would suit me to a T. Don't talk to me about comfort, I was never fussy in that department. To give you an idea, once during a Shriners' convention in Cleveland when every hotel in town was booked solid, I slept in the embalming lab of McAllister & Sons Funeral Parlor, in a coffin, and never knew a better night's rest."

"You were stretched out on my lawn when we met, so I don't think I caught your name."

Warren's surnames were mostly supplied by the telephone book, or the obituaries: Wadsworth, Wall, Walters, Waltham. There was a definite refinement to a name beginning with *Wa* that appealed to Warren's sense of dignity. *Wh* was another category he favored: White, Whitte, Whitman, Whittier—the poets—or painters, like Whistler (whose mother reminded Warren of his own). Some names he lifted from magazine ads and billboards, like Winston—or like Wingate, from nameplates in the foyers of fancy apartment buildings. Then there were the old standbys, tried and true, like Wilson, Wofford, Wright, Wyatt—and that was just the *W*'s alone. When young and just starting out—a fledgling, with energy to burn—the Abbots, Browns, and Chesterfields appealed to him, the A-B-C's so to speak. But waxing older, he was more and more inclined to assume an alias toward the end of the alphabet.

"Whitehead," said he, without blinking an eye. (In Citrus he was known as Wilson on one side of town and White on the other.) "Whitehead and Greenleaf—how's that for a colorful combination? I do believe we are going to get on together like hearts and flowers. And I wish you would call me Warren."

He would have given anything to see her expression at that moment, and might have risked kissing the back of her neck, or a convenient earlobe (had he not feared to go too far, too soon), but she was down on her knees sweeping up stray crumbs from beneath his chair into a silent butler.

Life, Lloyd, is a veritable paradise if you play your cards right.

Warren was already writing another "Dear Lloyd" letter in his head halfway through the crossword puzzle and Mrs. Greenleaf's last can of Seminole—a good thing the bathroom door was nearby, after all that beer. He could hear Mrs. G splashing around in her sunken *House & Garden* tub only ten steps away, submerged no doubt in a watery froth of perfumed bubbles, her silver tresses tucked into a shower cap.

He would be obliged to sleep in his underwear until he recovered his Gladstone from Miss Dowd's (he had neglected to mention Miss Dowd to Mrs. G, in case she had a jealous nature), but he recalled spotting an old safety razor in Mrs. Greenleaf's medicine cabinet—her late husband's last surviving memento. Something not many shavers know: you can always get two or three extra shaves out of an old blade by sharpening it on the inside of a water tumbler.

Meanwhile Warren had rigged a dandy bed lamp by tilting the Declaration of Independence lampshade on the spinning wheel to just the right angle for working crossword puzzles, and he had placed the chaise longue in the north-south axis so as to be in harmony with the earth's magnetic force.

Temporarily he was stuck on 17 Down: "—the _____ of kings," a quote from Shakespeare, not certain if the answer was "birth" or "death" since both were five-letter words and ended in *th*. Then he noticed that 36 Across was "Patron saint of lovers": Valentine, of course, which made *e* the second letter of 17 Down.

"Darned if you don't look like a valentine in that outfit," called out Warren as Mrs. Greenleaf flitted across the hall in a pink dressing gown down to her ankles. "For a minute I thought you were a king-size butterfly that somehow got in through the screen door."

She blushed the same color as her night garb and disappeared into the bedroom—but she would, Warren knew, be back.

It was a beautiful moment (except for the flowered shower cap on her head and the hot-water bottle under her arm), and Warren made a mental note to remember it, along with her endearing, "Sweet dreams," she had wished him earlier, when she showed him where to plug in the electric blanket—though he could not for the life of him see the need of an electric blanket in this climate.

Lloyd, I have always kept a backlog of such memorabilia in the back of my mind: satisfying strains of music, sonorous voices, snapshots of the passing parade . . .

Moments like this were the fleeting interludes of uplift others overlooked or allowed to slip away without an echo —but Warren was a rememberer. The past was as real as the present, and often more alive; the future was another tense he delighted in. When sequence went haywire and *tempus fugit* in all directions, he simply took a deep breath and swam with the tide on a wave of anticipation and nostalgia, a backwash of reminiscence superimposed on what was yet to be: the ruffles on his precious mother's quaint dustcap, for instance, or the taste of his next wife's first meatloaf forecast by the quality of ground beef she favored. Yes, the tableaux were sometimes farfetched: the sight of a colored gravedigger lowering himself into the grave he was digging, with the handle of a pick, like a gondolier's pole. ("Whose grave?" Warren yearned to ask him, when that particular vision flashed by), and a pretty girl's way with a piecrust—or her instep, if barefoot and unaware. A calliope piped a single note too shrill to endure. He heard a certain doctor's mellifluous diagnosis, saw a teenager's kneecap, tasted a glass of beer on Vine Street in Cincinnati when the head on a beer was three inches high. He saw a mushroom cloud at the end of the road at the same time as he recalled a blind beggar playing "Lady of Spain" on an accordion when he was courting Lillian, Lloyd's mother, and gave the old codger a dollar to impress her. (That was when a dollar was a dollar.) Classic earlobes, rolled silk hose, a drunk carrying a pumpkin, Wisconsin cheese on soda crackers, a vaudeville sketch at the Iroquois Theatre in Chicago so funny it made him cry. . . .

Warren was astonished to discover a teardrop had dampened Mrs. Greenleaf's monogrammed sheet, for he had not felt it coming.

Crossword puzzles of yore, certain tricky ones, he had unscrambled in the wee hours. (He sometimes worked a memorable crossword puzzle mentally, when no new crossword was at hand.) Over many a refreshing mug of beer, or during an inspired sunset in autumn, he could conjure up, apropos of nothing, the unforgettable odor of the upholstery in his faithful Hudson motorcar—or more often (too often, perhaps, for comfort) he would summon to his mind's eye the image of father and son on an excursion together aboard the *Island Queen,* and replay Lloyd's gesture from yesteryear waving his teddy bear at the toll booth on the Suspension Bridge. Steamboats still plied the Ohio in those days.

Although the edge of the sheet was wet with tears, Warren was far from melancholy. His sample case was near at hand, so he opened it and took out the prototype of that unique egg timer of his. If he could but explain to Lloyd how such moments as this quicken the blood, sweeten the sense, and darned near transport the spirit into realms of ecstasy. He set the miniature hourglass on the arm of his chaise longue but did not switch off the bedside lamp, knowing full well Mrs. Greenleaf was taking her nightgown off and putting perfume on and would return and beckon to him before the last grain of sand ran through.

The Circle Tour

M Y L O V E L Y N A ï V E L I A R has confessed. We are sitting on a café terrace in Cannes, with a view of the island where we met.

"I'm not who I pretend to be."

"Neither am I."

"Who did I say I was?"

On the Ile St. Honorat she told me she was a student journalist, and that her father was in the diplomatic service.

"Did I say that?" she asks unblinking, as if she cannot remember the lie among so many. "Sometimes I say Dad is a senator in the U.S. Senate. He's not. There's a real senator named Hughes, and when people know my name

is Hughes they think I'm the daughter of Senator Hughes.
I'm not."

I then ask what she expects me to ask: "Are you related
to the late Howard Hughes?"

"I've told people that, too. I said he was my uncle—but
that was before he died and looked so awful and they
revealed how kooky he was. So I stopped saying that.
Mostly, over here, I say I'm the daughter of an ambassador, and if people ask what country he's ambassador in I
say he's an ambassador-at-large."

At barely twenty (if that is her age) she still defines
herself by way of inventing a parent. I wonder (but do
not ask) if she means for me to be one of her fictitious
fathers.

"What does your father do, really?"

"He's dead."

"Oh. Sorry."

"Don't be. He died a long time ago. I don't know what
he did before he died because he was already divorced
from my mother and she didn't want to talk about him.
Maybe that's why I make up stories about who my
father is."

I, too, have lied to her. When she asked my age I
dropped seven of my thirty-seven years. I realize now the
truth would not have placed me in an unfavorable light,
or dissuaded her from doing what we inevitably did, but it
is too late to rid myself of the lie as easily as she sheds
hers. (Just as she so easily shed her clothing only hours
ago, on the island: this, in the childlishly direct way she
does everything, gracefully crosses her tanned legs, speaks
to the waiter in her college French, sips at a *citron pressé*
with less than a shrug of self-awareness.)

There is a monastery on the island, the chapel tower is
visible from here. It occurs to me the monks could have
observed us through the pines, but of course the monks

were at their prayers, or cultivating the fields of jasmine and lavender on the opposite side of the island. No such stricture entered my thoughts at the time. In her company, in our embrace, I was aware neither of witnesses nor of a generation gap.

I have come to accept that this girl has strayed into my orbit through no accident or act of will, but as the tagline of a prophetic joke.

"I told them at the film festival I wrote for *Harper's Bazaar.*"

"Do you?"

"I tried to get a job there as a receptionist once, but I didn't get it because I can't type. I've never really worked anywhere yet, I haven't written a line. But I figured, who knows the difference over here?"

"Did it work?"

"Like magic." She shows me a press pass for the Cannes Film Festival, a photograph of her smiling face attached. "It's only good for one person or I'd try to get you into the Palais."

She could not be more obliging, or decorative, had the Poet created her. Here is how he described her to me: "a sea creature, eyes wide as oysters." She is the very girl, and I have met her in exactly the way he said I would.

"Thanks. I'm not much into movies."

"What're you into?"

"I'm finishing a poem."

"Are you a poet?"

"The poem is by someone else. No, I'm no poet. My credentials are as bogus as yours. Listen."

The other patients refused to play Scrabble with the Poet. They said he made up words. (He did.) Also, his game of Monopoly was unorthodox and disrupting. If the Poet himself did not land on Mediterranean Avenue, he would go to any expense ("It's only play money, *mes amis,*") to wheedle that insignificant piece of real estate —along with its counterpart, Baltic—from the original owner. Then he would place a hotel on Mediterranean, and refuse to roll the dice when his turn came around.

"Why do you play Monopoly if you don't want to take your turn?"

"I've had my turn, Critic. Now I intend to rest on my laurels."

The Poet called me Critic. I was the arbiter of games at the Sans Souci, referee of the television set. (I decided which TV programs the patients might safely watch.) They came to me for playing cards, chess boards, and to be instructed in bridge and canasta and mah-jongg. I pronounced on the winning order of hands of poker, and decided if a Scrabble word was legitimate or not. I also provided books and magazines for the few patients who read, jigsaw and crossword puzzles for the fewer still who had the courage to work at puzzles.

It was I who reminded the Poet when he was scheduled for a shower, inquired about his bowel movements, and asked him not to circulate in the dayroom in his bathrobe.

"Who's circulating?"

"This is a mixed floor. It makes some of the women uneasy."

"Who's flashing the ladies? I've got my Fruit-of-the-Looms on underneath."

"Sorry." I tilted my head in the direction of his room.

"Don't be sorry," said he. "Never apologize. What would we do without you? It's you critics who steer us poets straight. Otherwise we wouldn't know what rules to play by, when to shock the ladies and when not. It's a critic's job to teach the rest of us right from wrong—right?"

He went along with me quietly enough, his voice low and apparently under control—but you never know what levels of rage lay behind a patient's offhand sarcasms. However, the Poet was passive enough to pass for one of ours, on the third floor, known informally as Passive City. On 4 and 5 the patients were segregated, male and female, to reduce the occasion (and excuse) for violence. But 3 was a mixed ward, where the patients were almost indistinguishable, in both manner and dress, from their visiting relatives. Passive City was a sanctuary for psychoneurotics and the elderly depressed, middle-aged schizophrenics who had settled into their disorders as if into an unhappy marriage, and an occasional teenage anorexic.

"Hang around while I change." He did not look at me in the eye when he said this, but at the name plate attached to my shirt pocket, possibly reading the word Critic there. "You can check me for scars."

He was referring obliquely to the evening he was admitted to the Sans Souci. Originally he had been taken to Mt. Sinai, on Miami Beach, then brought to the Sans Souci in a police ambulance, his hair and beard still wet. (Resuscitation was an emergency room procedure; Mt. Sinai had no psychiatric facilities, and no formal admission could be authorized.) I was on admissions duty at the Sans Souci when the Poet was brought in.

"Gandhi," he replied, when I asked his name, "Gandhi, with an h."

He did resemble a thin brown Gandhi (a bearded one) with his prominent skull and sunken eyes. He was wrapped in a blanket Mt. Sinai had provided (but requested that we return), and shoes without socks. Eventually he told me his real name, and I recognized it, though I am not a great reader of modern poetry. (I stocked a volume of his *Selected Poems* at a bookstore I once owned

—but I did not read the poems, or sell the book. When I later told him about my failed bookstore, the confession sealed a bond between us: partly because the enterprise had been a bookstore, partly because it was a failure.)

When he gave his address as "the cosmos," I did not immediately write it on his chart; I assumed he was being facetious.

"The Cosmos Motel, in Ft. Lauderdale. I kid you not."

He sloshed along beside me in his wet shoes and blanket to the shower room.

"A shower? I just had a bath in Biscayne Bay."

The Poet had been rescued by the Coast Guard when he attempted suicide by leaping from a tour boat near the Venetian Causeway.

"I'm afraid a shower is required on admission."

"You're afraid? I'm the one should be afraid. Listen, you know about Nazis inviting the likes of me to take a shower. What is this place, anyway? Sans Souci—you know what that means in French?"

"It means 'without care.' "

"A likely story. You know French?"

"No, I don't."

"Then how do you know what *sans souci* means?"

"That's what I've been told."

"Believe everything you've been told and you'll end up taking a shower when a Nazi asks you to."

In my three years at the Sans Souci I had pieced together a working personality of patience and forbearance. I waited.

"You're right," he said. "It does mean 'without care.' "

I adjusted the temperature of the water flowing from the shower head, and asked the Poet to disrobe.

"With you watching? Why can't that pretty nurse do this job?"

"Miss Ryan supervises the female admissions, I do the men."

"Why not the other way around?"

"Patients might get the wrong idea."

"Or the right idea."

But he let the blanket fall from his pathetically thin body, stepped out of his shoes and stood naked in the rising steam, the palms of his hands turned outward to show he had nothing to hide.

"What're you writing down?"

"I have to note any scars or identifying marks."

"The scars don't show. They're all on the inside."

I am lightheaded from a cloudy yellow apéritif called *pastis,* while Marybeth—intoxicated by something other than drink—sips at the last of her *citron pressé.* In her childlike way (for she is a child) she licks the spoon for the remaining lemony taste of sugar.

"You were into mental health, then?"

"I worked as a psychiatric aide at the Sans Souci Clinic in Sunny Isles."

"In Des Moines there's a funeral parlor called the Sans Souci."

"I can believe it."

For a moment the Poet himself occupies the third (but empty) chair at our café table.

"This poet doesn't sound all that kooky. After Howard Hughes died the way he did, I got to wondering if he wouldn't have been better off broke, and committed to an institution instead of hiding out in penthouses wearing Kleenex boxes on his feet—you know what I mean?"

"I do. But some of us—whether we're rich or poor, with or without the Kleenex boxes—have a way of committing ourselves, or being resigned, to long-term personal hells."

"I was into Transcendental Meditation once—would you believe it?"

"I would. I do."

After a four-day period of observation (including Rorschach tests, and the Wechsler-Bellevue), the Poet was diagnosed as Depressive Reaction, and placed on drug therapy. Dr. Poniatowsky warned the staff of the patient's suicidal impulsion and tendency to paranoia. I kept the Poet's razor, pen knife and nail file in a locked chest marked "Sharps." Because of his adverse effect on other patients (we had a minor flood on 3 when he told Mr. Marcus—an obsessive-compulsive who thought voices came through the water taps—that he would hear the voices more clearly if he left the faucets running), the Poet was assigned a private room at the far end of the corridor. At first he accepted what he called his "incarceration by narcosis" with the dazed resignation of the drugged—but his wit and whimsey surfaced soon enough.

"How long, legally or otherwise, can the Warden keep me in a helpless state of *sans souci*?"

The Poet referred to Dr. Poniatowsky as the Warden, or Freud's Afterbirth.

"These things take time."

"Is that a song by Cole Porter?"

"We've been trying to locate a relative, or someone responsible."

"To sign me in here, or sign me out? Why not allow me to decide if I want to be without care, or with. Irresponsible me. That's another song by Cole Porter."

"Is there somebody in your family—?"

"*Personne.* That's French for nobody—and also means somebody, just to confuse you students of French. I'm an orphan, a widower, an exile. Siblings, none. No next-of-kin since Keats died."

The Poet's sly hyperactivity was suspect. His energy (mostly verbal) did not correspond to the heavy dosage of anti-depressants Miss Ryan administered nightly. Dr. Poniatowsky advised a room search. To avoid possible paranoid accusations, the doctor suggested I make the inspection tour while the Poet was present. He stood by in his oversize Japanese kimono, making wry observations on my invasion of his privacy.

"Why do critics always insist there's more to a poet's baggage than meets the eye?"

In an attaché case, among the literary journals, books of poetry and notes for poems, I found a dozen books of matches inscribed with the crest of the Cosmos Motel. Matches were forbidden to patients, as the Poet well knew.

"I hate to ask you KGB thugs every time I want a light." He tightened his sash, shrugged, and surrendered to the philistines. "As a matter of fact, the poems you so cavalierly manhandled are more inflammatory than the matches."

I confiscated the matches without comment.

When I moved to the bed, he tried to distract me with a comic soft-shoe in his floppy slippers. "Cold," he advised, then danced to the window and shouted through the security screen: "Help! I've been kidnapped by a bankrupt bookseller!" I ran my hand beneath his mattress —"Cold, cold, cold,"—but then I removed a cigarillo tin, and he felt obliged to murmur, "Now you're getting warm."

The tin was full of the capsules Miss Ryan had dispensed to him for the last two weeks: a secret stash of multi-colored pills, unswallowed.

"I was saving them for a rainy day." He looked out through the security screen as if for rain.

Before I finished searching the bed, I came across a Kodachrome snapshot under his pillow. It was the photograph of a girl in her twenties, wearing jeans, a strand of her long hair windblown across the lower part of her face. She stood in profile beside a tan-and-white horse, her hand resting on the animal's neck.

"Please put that back." His voice had lost its mock-comic undertone.

He was right: I should not have picked up this personal memento, or examined it so indiscreetly. I replaced the photograph, face down, beneath the Poet's pillow.

"You get in touch with my wife," he said, "and I'll slit your throat."

Not all of his remarks were playful insults. But his razor, as I said, was locked in a box marked "Sharps."

"I thought his wife was dead."

"So did I. He called himself the Bleak Widower."

"She left him."

"Inevitably, yes. She was a student in his writing class at a university in Vermont. He was fifty-three, she was about your age, when they married."

"My father's not really dead," she suddenly confesses. "Why did I tell you that?"

"You want to know why I jumped? I was seasick, that's all. A case of *mal de mer*—with just a *soupçon* of *mal de siècle.* Can you commit a man to Bedlam because he was considerate enough of his shipmates not to vomit veal scallopini all over them? The Circle Tour, it was called— how could I resist? Captain Alighieri at the helm, with his lady friend Beatrice flipping the snap-tops on the Budweisers for him, and feeding him potato chips so he didn't have to take his tattooed paws off the wheel. The boat had a glass bottom you were supposed to watch the fishies through, but the glass needed a window-washing and I had lost a contact lens in a bowl of minestrone, so all I saw were the barnacle-encrusted beer cans imbedded in the sludge where Ali had tossed them overboard on previous tours—also the reflection of a ghastly green satanic visage (my own, as it turned out) floating through the subaqueous slime. Beatrice did the tourist spiel through the jeweled phallus of a microphone strung around her neck: 'Now passing Indian Creek Golf Course to starboard, folks, where famed pirate Bluebeard buried nine wives and came within a stroke of par on the tenth hole.' The 'folks' she referred to were yours truly, and the Dowds: Horace, age 68, three years retired from Akron Innertube, accompanied by Horabelle (Horace in drag) with a black umbrella resting on her puce bermudas like a coffin on a trestle. A discreet committee of thunderheads had gathered on the eastern horizon to threaten our circular voyage with the wrath of God, but I personally would have welcomed the downpour, or any heavenly baptism from on high—if that's what On High had in store for us. 'Why,' I asked Mrs. Dowd in all innocence, 'would anybody bring an umbrella to paradise?' Her scowl would have kept sharks at bay and her spouse raised his fishing rod as if to horsewhip me with it. Listen to the witnesses and I'll come out looking like a lunatic from the minute I stepped aboard, but consider a moment: is it sane to put forty-five years into innertubes so you can travel to Florida with Horabelle Dowd and her umbrella? Who's the lunatic here? And tell me, is it a madhouse offense to fall in love with a hand holding a can of Budweiser if the hand reminds you of a teeny-bopper's hand you once kissed? I wanted it to be me instead of Captain Neanderthal receiving the host of a potato chip on the tongue and thus entitled to lick the salt from those delicious fingers. My so-called psychiatrist is trying to convince me I was 'acting out' my nymphet wife's betrayal of me by rejecting my fellow passengers. As a doctor,

Dr. P would make a great poet. The truth is, I secretly lusted for a taste of our divine hostess' salted pinkies. Meanwhile Horace was trying to fish over the side of the boat but all he caught was the other side of the boat, and his wife (who truly resembled J. Edgar Hoover) was offering me vitamin B out of her beach bag for my 'nerves.' (You're yawning behind that hand, Critic.) True, the scene was *boring,* as my students used to say about poetry, college, life. My adrenaline wasn't even up. But I allowed impulse to override common sense. (That's how I got married, by the way.) I snatched Mrs. Dowd's umbrella, aimed it at Alighieri, then leaned into Bea's cleavage and shouted into her mike: 'Remain in your places, everybody —this is a hijack. Above all, don't panic. Captain, take this tub to St. Tropez!' Ali's knotted brow looked like a pile of anchor chain, but Beatrice, I will always believe, was secretly smiling, if only in her soul. I mean, here was destiny's tot, surrounded by hostiles on a glass boat circling Miami Beach, only an umbrella to defend myself—what would *you* do? I jumped."

For the first time, in the Poet's presence, I smiled—an unprofessional lapse on my part.

"The funny thing was, I really did want to go to St. Tropez."

The smile gave me away. My passkey to Passive City lost all significance: whatever further authority I might pretend to exercise had been un ¹ermined by that smile. In one careless moment of natural rapport, the Poet and I became friends, an impossible conspiracy between keeper and kept.

"Tell me the truth, Critic. Didn't you, all your life, want to go to the south of France?"

"Yes," I confessed.

"Like me, you came to Florida as a cut-rate substitute for the real thing, for the Mediterranean."

"I never thought of it that way."

"Unhappily married, right?"

I was no longer smiling, but I said, "Yes."

"Same miserable hangups, both of us—so how come you can tell me when to take a shower, and I can't even light my own cigarettes?"

"I didn't jump overboard."

"That may be your problem."

So much of our fragile commitment originates on her side: it is Marybeth who takes my hand, not I hers. We stroll through the flower market at the foot of a steep street leading to the cathedral and ramparts of an older Cannes. We are on our way to her hotel—I will call it the Mediterranean (mine is the Baltic, only a few steps away)—so that she might change for a gala *soirée* at the Palais des Festivals. Fishermen in blue undershirts play *boules* in the dust alongside the yacht basin: they do not look up from their measurements as a biplane flies quite low over their game trailing a banner that announces tonight's film. A flower seller thrusts a bouquet of carnations at us. I remember the Poet saying, "Buy her flowers," and I exchange a ten-franc note for the bouquet so that Marybeth might dip her flower face into the flowers. In the next instant she unclasps her hand from mine to count the blossoms.

"Thirteen," she announces, a shadow across her oyster eyes.

"Are you superstitious?"

"I don't know. I do know a black umbrella brings bad luck."

"But not thirteen carnations. If you counted them, saying, 'He loves me, he loves me not,' a dozen would have been the unhappy number."

"I never thought of it that way."

The reward for having thought of this is to see her smile again.

"I'm not all that superstitious, but I shouldn't have told you my father was dead. How would I feel if he really did die?"

"What does your father do, really?"

"Oh, he's got an office somewhere, where he makes money. He gives me money. He gave me money to come over here, look." She maneuvers around the carnations to extract a booklet of traveler's checks from her jeans. The checks are in one-hundred-dollar denominations, but I do not count them as she did the flowers. The book of checks is to prove that her father exists.

Satisfied that our relationship has now been launched on a course of strict candor, she puts the checks back into her pocket where they make a secure bulge against her thigh. She takes my hand again—her child's hand grasping two fingers of mine—as we resume our stroll. The late sun eases behind a range of red cliffs called l'Estérel, and she tilts her head to catch the last glimpse, or warmth, of it.

"I don't feel guilty taking money from him. He ran out on Mom and me, didn't he?"

A breeze from the sea sweeps a strand of her hair across the lower part of her face. I am reminded of a face in a photograph, but she does not resemble the girl the Poet loved, only the girl he invented.

"Guilt is the good doctor's cover story for all my sins of omission, or emission. When I ask the Warden, 'Why should *I* feel guilty?—she's the one who ran out on me,' he's the cocktail-party pedant who paraphrases your question by way of a cute answer: 'Zen vy do you veel guilty?' Listen, that lovely naïve liar of mine told me the guy was her *brother,* hitchhiked all the way from Colorado just to visit Sis. I had a night class that night and like an idiot laid thirty bucks on them, my blessing, to go to a disco together. I never saw her again. Turns out the hitchhiker was some apprentice guru she was once at a be-in in Denver with—no relation whatsoever, except sexual. Truth may be beauty, *mon ami,* but beauty is *not* truth. My beard she declared was so 'adorable' during the courtship she asked me to shave off on our honeymoon because it made me look 'ancient.' O.K., I take into consideration her grotesque childhood, trundled from barracks to barracks by Major-Daddy Warmonger, surrounded by slavering GI's all her young life. (Mommy went AWOL when the kid was still in kindergarten.) Picture her in her first bikini, already overripe at fourteen, enticing whole platoons of volunteers for fatigue duty in Major-Daddy's back yard during sun-bath afternoons, trim hedges for a better look, mow her lawn for her, apply Lan-o-Tan if necessary. Put yourself in my place. A pedagogue's wet dream transfers from Camp Pendleton to Pendennis College and asks the Poet in Residence to look at some 'little things' of hers after class. I looked. That extracurricular peek cost me tenure. (I'm not saying she wasn't worth it.) The Committee on Promotions referred to the episode as 'unwarranted involvement with the student body.' Who warrants these things? I read her puerile poetry, got involved with her student body, and fell in love with her—in that order. Guilt does not appear in the indictment, Critic—anguish, yes."

The question was, had anguish swept him over the side of a tour boat; was the Poet deranged in the way we think of as clinical? Miss Ryan probed his mouth with a tongue depressor ("Last time," she told me, "he tried to lick my fingers") to make certain he really did swallow his bedtime capsules. Would that I had probed past his madcap monologues, listened for the ventriloquist's voice behind his verbal high jinks.

"Ve vill now discuss anguish as a vay of life." His impersonation of Dr. Poniatowsky included an Eastern European accent the doctor did not have.

Yes, I succumbed to what I considered his charm. He inquired about my wife, I told him about her. At first I may have been evasive, or tried to change the subject, but eventually I traced my circle along the milestones of a sterile marriage. Institutional protocol had broken down. The Poet had acquired access to my case history, the roles of patient and attendant were reversed.

"Talk about guilt. Ever occur to you, Critic, that you may be more your wife's problem than she is yours?"

"I feel responsible for her."

"Who feels responsible for you?"

However helpless he may have been against his own malaise, he could apply the neurotic's shrewd intuition to mine.

"She once tried to commit suicide."

"Haven't we all?"

He had conspired to make me smile again, but I replied in all seriousness: "I couldn't take the chance."

"Meanwhile," he sighed, "it suits you to commit slow suicide playing parlor games with the crazies."

My answer was absurd: "I can live with it."

He nodded his shaggy head in resignation, not agreement. Suddenly, as if to discover how many games I did know how to play, he asked me if I had ever been to Calder, a race track in Miami.

"I'm not much into racing."

"Of course not," said he. With his back turned to me he produced a racing form from among the literary quarterlies in his attaché case. He showed me a name encircled by magic marker: "Ever hear of a horse named Naiad?

Never mind. Nor would you have sullied your virgin thoughts with a villanelle entitled *Naiad* written by guess-who? about a naiad in the flesh. (By the way, she once said to me, 'If children commit adultery, shouldn't it be called infantry?' Any wonder I fell in love with her?) Therefore you would not have discerned fate's negligent irony in running my runaway naiad in the seventh race at Calder tomorrow."

"No," I confessed.

From between the pages of his *Selected Poems* he drew forth a dozen twenty-dollar bills. I had not thought to examine the volume when I searched his room: patients were not permitted to keep money or valuables in their possession.

"It's only play money, *mon ami.*"

He advised me to play the ponies, play poet for a change, then placed the sheaf of twenties in my hand.

It is Marybeth's idea to leave the shower curtain open so that I might watch her at her bath. How right the Poet was (among other things) about the ideal complement of sexes in the *salle de bains.* I study her body as if to memorize it, but I do not search for scars.

"If it was a movie," she says through the water-spray, "the horse would have to win."

My delight in her is constant. I will be as pleased to see her in evening dress as in jeans, or in the nude. "A heart-breaker," the Poet promised me, "with hair down to here."

"What is the movie tonight?" I ask.

"A western. Only it was made in Italy."

I will be waiting for her on the steps of the Palais. When she emerges from the dark into the light of arc lamps on the Croisette, I will know from the look in her oyster eyes if the ending was happy or not.

"What did your wife say when you said you were taking off?"

"The Poet was right about her, too." Marybeth has shut off the water, I shout into an unexpected silence: "All those years," then lower my voice, "she had been seeing somebody—somebody else."

This last is a lie. I did not tell my wife I was leaving her. All candor is on Marybeth's side now; I have become the liar-at-large. Guilt did not appear in the indictment against the Poet, but guilt—when I take the time to brood about my cowardice—is part of the indictment against me. The Poet promised me a place, and a girl in that place—he did not name the price I must pay for an escape from Passive City.

But I want this girl to take childish pleasure in the moment just as I, selfishly, take my pleasure in her. I want her to have happy endings. For that reason I end my story with the sum of our winnings at Calder. (I won only half as much as the Poet, for I had only half his faith in precognition.) I cannot tell her the entire truth, or carry my tale to its unhappy conclusion.

When I came on duty that night, with money in my pocket for him, the Poet was not in the dayroom making Scrabble and Monopoly miserable for his fellow patients. At the door to his room I felt his death before I entered. (The dead—contrary to scientific proof—do give off an aura.) With the sash to his kimono he had hung himself from the shower head, and dangled there in the gruesome rigidity that follows the cessation of all vital functions.

He had managed to conceal one last book of matches from his careless guardian, for the wash basin contained the ashes of papers he had destroyed, perhaps a photograph among them. The note he left was addressed to me: "Finish my poem for me, Critic."

House of the Blues

WALKING THE PONT NEUF I walked past the old Vert Galant statue all slimy green wet in the rain—but he's brass and won't get warped like a guitar will, or melt, like me. Tried to poke my guitar up under my army surplus jacket but no go, me and it just got all the wetter. Didn't it rain? Here I was, out in the freezing French rain trying to locate my buddy Roger-D Rogers who wasn't nowhere to be found. Roger-D was the one that first give me the money to go down to Spain on. He's got some prostitute works for him—about the best-pay job you can get in Paris. I was just back from my travels and broke again. Maybe old Rog—if I could find him—would let me have franc number one, to get me started. All I wanted was money enough to get dried off someplace. April in Paris, Jesus.

It was like I was some kind of private eye out looking all over Paris for this missing person. What you do, you *cherchez la femme* first, like a detective would, but I already walked up and down rue Saint-Denis twice and couldn't find a woman in a doorway anywheres. Back before I went to Spain, rue Saint-Denis was the town's reddest red-light street—flower faces blooming at every café window, birds chirping their price at street corners, butterflies flitting along the curbside ready to wrap you up in their silky wings. Just reach for your wallet, you had your pick.

But Paris getting cleaned up of late. Government's out scraping the gray off the house fronts, cops'll bust the first girl says, *"Tu viens?"* to you in public. From the looks of things, Roger's woman wasn't the only one missing in action. A whore street turned into a cemetery. What's the use of nice clean buildings if you can't have Paris's best-looking women standing out in front of them?

Figured I'd try his old hotel on rue de la Harpe, but I didn't have any confidence of him still there. People I been acquainted with don't stay any too long at the same hotel—and addicts, like Roger, never leave their forward addresses. I went over there anyway, soaked to the bone by the time I ducked in the lobby. Nobody behind the desk. That was lucky for me or I'd've got chased out for dripping rainwater all over their downstairs carpet.

I climbed up five flights, tough climbing waterlogged as I was. He used to live next door to the WC so I held my breath when I knocked. The door finally opened a crack, but no Roger. It was Lulu, his prostitute.

Right away the door started shutting closed again. My color gets you a poor reception at people's doors. Lucky I got my surplus army boot in before she got the door all the way shut.

"*N'est pas là,*" she told me, one evil eye looking out through the crack.

"I'm his buddy that went to Spain." I said that so she wouldn't think I was the cops. "I'm back."

"*Fous-moi le camp,*" she said, which means bug off.

"I'm the one brought you that package that time, remember?"

She opened the door half a centimeter off my big toe. You could see her other eye. She studied me a minute, mean, and finally remembered.

"You owe him some money, is what I remember."

"No I don't. He give me that money."

She opened the door some more—all the way the chain would go—and stuck her whole face out at me.

"How much he give you? What was he giving you money for? We're broke, he needs that money."

"Well, I'm broke myself. He give me that money to keep. I did him a job and he paid me. He said to take a package over to you that night and I took it and he paid me the money to do it."

"How much he give you?"

Women, when they get on the subject of money, you can't budge them. Especially whores.

"Hundred francs."

"Hundred *francs?*" Her pencil eyebrows shot up. Her big painted eyes got twice as big. "He could've hired an armored car for a hundred francs. That was just a *note* he sent over to me, with some *chocolate* in it."

"How did I know what was in it?" said I, acting like I never knew what was in it. (The note said, "*Je t'aime,*"

165

three times, wrapped around a chocolate bar.) "I thought it was dope and I was taking a big risk to carry it around Paris."

"*Risk?* That wasn't no risk. That was *chocolate* in that package."

"Well, Roger never told me what it was. I thought he was dealing, and it was dope."

"Roger's off dope."

I didn't answer nothing to that. I believe that when I see it.

"He's off dope and gained four kilos. We got married January seventh and I've took care of him since."

You could've knocked me over with a broomstraw. She stuck her hand out over the door chain to show me her wedding ring. It was true. The hinges went out of my jaw. I should've knew something was up the minute I first sneaked a look in that hotel room. Everything was all changed around from the last time I saw Roger. Somebody painted the place lemon color with a linoleum with roses on it on the floor. There was a stuffed chair in there now, with doilies all over it to hide the cigarette burns, and a new brass bed from the flea market where Rog's cot used to be. Shelves all over the place with knickknacks from Monoprix on them and a red-white checkerboard oilcloth on the table with a goldfish bowl with two goldfish in it. Lulu had even put up polka-dot curtains on the airshaft window. Whores are great that way for interior decoration.

You can't argue with a wedding ring. There sat the evidence on Lulu's finger—Roger-D Rogers had went and married his prostitute and lost hisself a good income.

When I could work my mouth again I said, *"Tiens, tiens,"* meaning, "My, my," or something just as foolish, and that's when she took advantage and put a spike heel down hard on my big toe and got the door slammed shut. Damn. And I didn't even find out where Roger was at.

"Wait a minute! Where's he gone to?"

I could hear her through the door: "He don't see no-body but me. He's in a hospital and he's gained back four kilos already."

"But I'm his best buddy—"

"Fous-moi le camp."

That was a very careless hotel for Paris because some-body had went and forgot to put the lock on the down-stairs telephone dial. So I sneaked behind the front desk like I belonged there and called up. I called up this Amer-ican lady very big with different organizations like Moral Rearmament and the SPCA. Somebody come on in French and I asked for Madame Price-Loftus and they said, *"Ne quittez pas,"* and then somebody else come on in English.

"Good afternoon. This is Miss Beardsley, secretary to Mrs. Price-Loftus. May I help you?"

I told her who I was. I said Mrs. P-L told me to call up if ever I needed help, and I was broke right now and needed help.

"Excuse me, but do you happen to be of Afro-American extraction?"

Nice of her to excuse herself. I could've said no, as easy as not, but I just said, "I'm black"—honest as day-light.

"I'm terribly sorry, but on March third of this year Mrs. Price-Loftus was set upon by two Negroes at the inter-section of rue des Pyramides and avenue de l'Opéra. A report of this regrettable episode appeared in the Paris *Herald-Tribune*—"

"I been away."

"—cut and bruised and only spared further, and more serious, injury by the fortunate intervention of a passerby. She was robbed of her purse and a double strand of matched pearls, the latter of considerable sentimental value. Mrs. Price-Loftus has since withdrawn all aids and supports from any nonwhite individuals as well as organizations purporting to represent these individuals."

I started to argue it could have been Arabs—white people never pay attention to different shades of dark—but the telephone had already went click.

This other buddy of mine, André, lived in a beat-up old barge tied up next to the Piscine de Ligny, which is an actual swimming pool right out in the Seine. André made a steady living stealing suitcases out of cars parked around the gare de Lyon. He was home, because I passed his rusty motor scooter chained to a dock post and there was smoke coming out of his smokestack.

Inside was wet clothes hanging all over everyplace and the portholes shut and André sitting in front of the coal stove wringing out socks in a bucket of river water. As soon as he sees me he dropped his socks and came over and give me a big French bear hug full of Supersuds.

"When you back in Paris, man? Hey, that's the greatest, see your ugly *gueule* again. Like man it's a switch to see a mug with a smile on. Ever since Saturday *flics*'re out to finger me for heisting tires off army trucks at Invalides. *Truck* tires, can you feature me jacking up army trucks to steal their tires off? I ain't even got a jack, and Invalides ain't my territory."

That's the way he talked, only he couldn't pronounce nothing right. He talked American and wanted to go to America in the worst way and be a gangster, on account of seeing too many movies.

". . . got bour-glar alarums built into every damn *deux chevaux,* so help me Jesus, that you turn on air-raid sirens to try and jimmy an honest window. Sweetcases is for the birds *moment-aire*—what I got to do is switch into bigger meat or go bust."

He was hopping barefoot around stacks of empty jimmied-open suitcases, popping mothballs into pockets of suit coats hanging on hangers amongst the wetwash. Claimed fences knocked twenty francs off the payoff for bugholes.

"Twenty francs, so help me Jesus."

Asked him why he didn't just quit and go legit.

"Got to make my bundle, man, before I blow this town."

Since he was on the subject of bundles I figured I could hit him for a friendly little loan, say fifty francs—but all he come up with was ten.

"Sorry, man, my overhead's way up since Françoise talk me into *volontaire* join-up with *sécurité sociale*. She gets to get rid of that baby we damn near had, would've cost a bundle for *avortement privé* only now *sécurité sociale* is paying."

Françoise was his girl that wrote poetry in her spare time.

"Only now we got to pay *sécurité sociale* first."

The ten he give me smelt of mothballs, but it was ten more than I come in with, so I pocketed it.

Asked him if he heard any news about Roger-D Rogers.

"Cat's had it, man—married his *poule* to keep from being a *maquereau*."

"Yeah, I met the little lady herself. She said she put Rog in a hospital where he's getting cured and I'm trying to locate where the hospital's at."

"Drug cure, it's the Maison Bleue. They put all the dips in the Maison Bleue. Bughouse hospitals, they're all out in Vincennes."

The Maison Bleue, so that was where Roger-D Rogers was at. Used to be a jazz piano player, you know. Rog played very cool piano for a white boy, very cool. But he was way downhill last time I saw him. Downhill and still rolling. Wondered if Lulu'd really put him back on his feet again, in a hospital bed at the house of the blues.

André give me a bowl of coffee black as me, made out of river water—but the Seine is OK if you boil it first. I sat down on an empty steamer trunk stuck with labels from all over the universe and sucked my brew. Then André handed me a pair of rusty shears and asked me if I'd haircut his hair around back where he couldn't reach it. He said Françoise liked him long-hair and wouldn't cut it, but there was a mug shot of him at the *préfecture* with his hair long.

"We'll fox the cops," said he. "Make me look like Cagney, make me look like George Raft."

You couldn't make André look like anybody except Aznavour, but I chopped away at his hair while he looked in a looking glass, trying to keep the hair out of my coffee.

After I dusted his shoulders off like a porter in a barbershop, I asked him casual: "Was wondering if you happen to have a spare bed I could sleep on tonight on the boat someplace."

Shook his shaggy haircut no, sorry as hell: "—but Françoise my girlchick coming by tonight. You dig?"

French people are shyer about privacy than you'd think, but I don't blame them.

Over on the Right Bank by the Samaritaine Department Store the *clochards* were sleeping out on the subway gratings, covered over with copies of *l'Humanité,* which is about all the good a Paris bum ever gets out of a Communist newspaper. I almost wished I could crawl in there with them. The rain already quit raining and there's always a nice warm steam comes up out of the *métro* tunnel. But there's no room for me, and anyway I don't want to get caught sleeping under *l'Humanité.* FBI see me, I'd end up with my passport took away.

What I wanted was to find my sculptor buddy Marcel that worked at les Halles and slept in the back of a cheese wholesale house, maybe I could sleep in there with him. I slept there once before, it's nice. Cheeses big as cotton bales and Marcel's sculptures he makes out of tomato crates and you go to sleep like a mouse smelling gruyère and port salut and eat cheese and bread for breakfast in the morning.

Les Halles was all lit up with spotlights so the unloaders could see to unload by, and all around was crates of spinach and celery leafs sticking out of the slats and big neat pyramids of melons trucked up from the springtime south (where I should've stayed, instead of coming home to freeze my ass in Paris) and artichokes and whole piles of grapefruit—mountains of them—waiting to be sorted for size. Those hefty les Halles ladies in their half a dozen sweaters and wearing rubber boots was out hosing down seeds and peelings where the rotten stuff was tossed to one side, and beggars with ratty shopping bags went picking through the mounds of ruint oranges to go and try to sell them to poor people tomorrow, and the thickest-built huskies I ever saw east of the U.S. waterfront out hauling crates and treeloads of bananas on their backs with burlap shoulder pads to soak up the sweat, their big fat faces straining tomato color under the weight, and hot-breath steam clouds blowed out in the cold where they heaved and hauled, setting up the Paris France dinner table under the spotlights.

There was fires built around to stop and get warm at. I went over to a bonfire of splintered-up crate wood in an oil drum to ask some biddy roasting her fingers if she saw Marcel lately. She said no, she didn't know him, and to ask this guy sitting in his truck across the street by the sheds, he knew everybody.

He was reading *France-Soir* newspaper murders under the big lights.

"Artist-type, *n'est-ce pas?*"

I said *oui.*

"Carves out statues in the daytime, right?"

I said right, said he only worked nights hauling fruit.

"Curly-headed kid trying to grow a mustache?"

I said that's right, that's him.

"Drafted."

Drafted? Marcel drafted into the army? What they want with sculptors in the military for?

"Send him off to fight Turks someplace, or Esquimaux." He flipped back to his *France-Soir,* fed up with the world. "That's the goddamn government for you."

And Roger-D Rogers married to a whore, in a hospital, and André wanting to go to America. Seemed like all my best civilized buddies gone down the drain.

Just then the sky popped open and a cloudburst of crystal marbles fell down out of the black instead of rain. Right on top of everybody. Hailstones big as mothballs, bouncing around hard and beaning everybody. And *sting,* Jesus. People looked up from their fruit stacks to see what hit them. I ducked across the street to St. Eustache church, hailstones pelting hell out of me all the way across.

St. Eustache was still open, some old people inside praying late. I could still hear hailstones rattling against the church windows, so I stayed inside, out of it. Pretty soon the guard come by running people off, right in the middle of their beads.

I hid off in a corner behind a statue of St. Somebody in the shadows, out of the candlelight, and stayed there and the guard never saw me, passed me right by. Then I saw somebody else come by, janitor or somebody, so I ducked behind a curtain and found myself in a confession box, so I sat me down.

It had a little window with bars, like a jail cell, where you talk through to a priest—or where the priest talks through to you. I wasn't sure whether I was sitting on the confess side or the forgive. All I know is it smelt of onions and general halitosis in there—but it was halfway warm, and as private as you can get. I listened and heard the guard shut the big heavy front door shut and slam the bolt home. Then he shuffled down the stone walkways turning out lights, snuffing candles, shutting the incense off and such last-minute chores and closing-time stuff till he shuffled on up some stone steps someplace, just his echoes all over the whole entire church, then quiet.

I sneaked a peek out the curtain.

Lights all turned off except some rows of little candles set in red jars to keep from setting the place on fire, and some big candles stuck on spikes that signify bigger sins than the little candles. A candle is a prayer for somebody dead and gets you out of hell faster if it burns steady. While I was looking, one of the candles ran out of wax and went out. Tough shit, I think that goes on your record. I had a pack of *Gauloises* André give me and was dying for a smoke, but damnit, no light. So I finally sneaked out quick and quiet and took a light off somebody's candle. They wouldn't know the difference.

It does make you think back on your sins to be sitting in a confession box, locked up in a church, smoking a *Gauloise bleue*. But thinking about everything I ever did wrong and summing up my backlogs of evil deeds finally put me to sleep. Lucky my cigarette went out before I did, or I would've gone up in smoke and the box been my coffin.

Next thing I knew three big tremendous organ-pipe

notes rocked me and St. Eustache awake both. Organ player'd come in to practice. Daylight was coming through the color windows.

To get to the *Maison Bleue* you take a *métro* train at Châtelet and go all the way to the end of the line at Vincennes and then you find out you got to take a bus the rest of the way. There's different hospitals out there named the Rose House and the White House and all, and I had to get the right bus for the Blue House.

Green lawns all around with spider-leg sprinklers and flower gardens started where when the weather got better some flowers would spell out MB, for *Maison Bleue,* but right now it was only dried stalks and buds and a few new leaves.

The hospital was back behind a high wall trimmed all along the top with broken bottle glass to cut your hands to pieces if you tried to climb over. I don't know if it was to keep people out or keep people in.

Bicycles and parked cars parked sidewise against one wall and people going through the gate carrying get-well candy and flowers and clean laundry, and I was glad I had sense enough to remember to bring old Roger some fruit I bought cheap at les Halles out of André's ten francs.

A guard in a little stone concierge house told me which building to go to, Building B, and a nun met me at Building B with a string of keys tied around her waist instead of a crucifix. She unlocked for me to go into a white hallway. I followed her down the hall to another door where she talked through a peephole to somebody until that door opened up and there was a nurse, all starched up, waiting. I said who I wanted to see and the nurse let me in and the nun stayed outside. The system was something on the line of Alcatraz.

Everything was white-white-white—white walls and ceilings, white lights hanging down, and white enamel beds with white sheets over them. Like to snow-blinded me. I was the only shadow in the whole place.

Two rows of beds like in the army, with mostly old men sitting on them and the visitors sitting next to the beds on stools or standing around leaning against the white walls talking. When you got up close you saw it wasn't all that clean as it was white. I noticed where the paint was chipped off the enamel beds and saw slop jars poked out from under the mattresses. Down at the far end of the bed row was Roger-D Rogers hisself, sitting in bed propped up on a pillow with an old guy sitting next to him, playing checkers with him.

I gave a yodel and went down to handshake him but all he said was, "Well. Look who came down to see Roger-D in his sick bed. My ace number one favorite guitar player, back from España, never even sent me a postcard."

With Roger you never knew if he was glad to see you or wished you were dead or what.

"Came all the way out here to our quaint nuthouse to play us folks a folk song."

I was carrying my guitar with me on account of I didn't have no safe place to leave it at. Everything he said, he always said it sarcastic—Rog never liked to let down on his cool. It didn't mean nothing personal. He always called me a folksinger to try and get my goat. But I made up my own songs, and played them, and he knew it.

Yes, it was the same old Roger-D for put-on and put-down but he was changed a lot in the face, blowed up twice his previous size like he was in 3-D for a change. I told him how good he looked and he turned the good word aside with a wrist flip.

"I'm off Stuff, you know. I'm cured from that scene."

Benny, horse, hash, big O—all that stuff—he called it Stuff.

"I saw Lulu yesterday, I heard."

"They got this new addict treatment they call the *cure de sommeil*. They put you to sleep and feed you through a hose. You only wake up once a day to go to the crapper. The rest is sweet dreams, baby. They keep giving you shots of something. You never feel a thing. You're asleep. Doc talks to you while you're under and tells you what a famous guy you are, to build back your confidence." He started fingering thin air, playing the whole story out for me, like playing piano. "That's my exact problem, you know—lost confidence in myself. Lulu read about the treatment in the French *Reader's Digest* and found out a doctor to do it and signed me in here instead of us going on a honeymoon. I'm a goddamn new man."

He stopped moving his fingers at me and held his hand out over the top of the checkerboard to show me how steady he was. Looked to me like it still shook anyway, but he was a hell of a lot better, I admit.

I noticed the old guy just sitting there listening to us talk English, polite, not making a sound, so I said in French, "Don't let me bust up your checker game."

The old guy smiled at me with his mouth open and I saw where he didn't have tooth one, just a lot of gums and an old man's big old tongue. He went on smiling like that till he drooled down on his hospital pajamas. That's the trouble with old men, they start smiling too long at a stretch.

"Don't pay any attention to Checkers. He's nuts, you know." Roger was still holding his hand out to show me how steady it was. "I play checkers with the bastard to keep him happy. He makes my moves for me and I play all his for him."

Old Checkers nodded and drooled and moved one of Rog's red checkers to show me how.

"Whores always make the best wives, you know," says Rog, out of the blue, hand still out trying to show me how steady a hand a whore makes you, too. "Look at that hand, would you?"

Me and Checkers looked some more.

"That's the sleep treatment does that, you know."

Roger kept saying "you know" all the time every time he said anything, which gets monotonous but keeps you up answering.

"That's an awful steady hand," said I, and the old boy nodded and held *his* hand out for good measure. It was steadier than Roger's if you ask me.

Then he finally put his hand down and the old man did the same and they both belched a little gas like twins that had the same dinner.

"Food's lousy here."

Which reminded me what I brought. I heaved my sack of pears and cherries up onto Rog's bed.

"What the hell's that?"

"Just some fruit. Figured you might like to taste some fresh fruit, fresh right out of les Halles."

Roger smiled his tricky jazzman smile at me and said, sly, "You didn't by any chance smuggle some Stuff in there in that bag, did you?"

I smiled back and said, "No. Just fruit."

Roger chuckled way low in his belly and acted relaxed and said, "I'm off Stuff, you know."

Old man backed him up, nodding yes.

"That's what Lulu told me. Congratulations." I was congratulating for the cure, not Lulu.

I noticed where he went pawing through the pears and sorting cherries looking careful for any kind of little surprise that could maybe turn out to be Stuff. Then when he

saw all there was was just fruit he smiled a different way
and reached in and give me and the old man each a pear.
He didn't eat none of it, hisself.

There was a long spell of quiet with just me and Checkers munching pear and all around us visitors buzz-buzzing
in different patients' ears and somebody way off in Solitary
someplace screaming regular as heartbeat, to remind you
what kind of a hospital we were at—but it was far enough
off you didn't take it too personal. Then Roger-D asks
me, "You still banging hell out of that banjo?"

"Yeah"—it was a guitar, and he knew it—"still."

"You're nuts, you know that?"

"Can't help it."

"Yes you can, man. You can wise up and quit. Look at
me. I quit, didn't I?"

Never had no sermons out of Roger-D Rogers before,
so I just listened and never said a word back.

"I'd still be nuts back playing piano, shooting Stuff and
dying out by inches the way I was. You saw me, how I
used to be when I was hung up on H, and music. But I
found how to quit, didn't I? I'm a new goddamn man."

He was, too. Put on some baby fat under the eyes and
he had an extra chin to rest his face on. His hair was
mostly all gone, but what was left was neat combed with
a neat shave to back it up. Nurse or somebody, maybe
Lulu, clipped his fingernails down clean for him, had him
smelling like Lysol and after-shave.

Sure, he had a wife now, too, and a bird-nest hotel
room with curtains on the window to go home to when
he went home out of the *Maison Bleue.* The man was fat-
ter and more sassy than I ever saw him before. You could
even picture him sometime maybe up and have kids, and
be a father like regular people. I wouldn't put nothing
past him—that's how brand-new hospital changed and
dry-cleaned he was.

The old man was quiet reaching in the sack for cherries and slipping them between his gums, swallowing cherry stones and stems and all. While Checkers was working on the cherries Roger-D leaned over to me and whispered, confidential, like he wanted to keep the old man out of it, "I'm really off Stuff for life, you know. I'm to where I could even take a little pinch now and then, maryjane or something mild, and get the good of it, and have a little Technicolor once in a while, and let up whenever I want, and quit right after. I mean I can *handle* it now, you understand what I mean?"

His eyebrows went all up into wrinkles looking question marks at me, wanting me to back him up. "I was one time a famous guy, you know—" he whispered behind his fingers, even his fingers was fat, those same fingers that used to be thin as pretzels and played the furtherest-out jazz piano in Parisville. There was little driblets of honest-to-god tears in the man's eyes when he said to me, "So what do I need Stuff for?"

I had to look out the window and watch the sprinklers. White people are like innocent little kids when they're like that. When I never said nothing and couldn't look him in the eye he must've knew I knew. He saw I saw right through him.

Reached out, pissed-off, and took the sack away from the old man and took a pear to eat.

"When you going to wise up and shut down that stupid music box of yours?"

He was off goofballing again, tears dried, sarcastic mouth full of pear.

"I like guitar."

Poked the old man with his elbow, winking at him. "He *likes* guitar for chrissake." Then back to me, "God-damn amateurs are coming in the windows. *Folk*singers crawling out of the woodwork, working *métro* stations with their hat out, cluttering up the profession."

Roger-D Rogers could switch from buddy-buddy to bastard quicker'n anybody I ever saw. I knew I wasn't no Andy Segovia, but I wasn't no amateur neither. OK, I was never known to the general public like him, but my music was purentame me, without no Stuff to prop it up.

"Guitar's all I know."

"Learn something. Learn shoeshine or be a bellboy—make yourself an honest buck. You never get anywhere in music, you know that, don't you? Look at me, and I was *good*."

He was, too.

"If you want to bang guitar, bang it private and don't go messing around the shitting public. Public's a killer. Public'll whip your ass and put you in a straitjacket to cure you from living, like they did me."

Spit his pear out all over the checkerboard to try and vomit the public up. His face turned blue from being so hateful and he had to scratch his neck with both hands where it was a blotchy red rash, and itched.

I kept quiet and shut up. Old man cleaned up where Rog'd spit out pear, sad to see a good pear wasted. Anything you said would only work him up worse.

But all of a sudden he calmed down to earth and his eyes went glassy staring down the bed rows where a door opened up, and it was Lulu. She strutted onstage with every man-jack's eyeballs on her, she was used to it.

Her dress was plain enough but she was strapped into it real tight, and she had went all out on makeup to make up for the dress being only black and white. Legs were all hard muscle from standing around Saint-Denis so many years, with black fishnet stockings on them. Her hair was standing up on end where some madman must've back-combed it with a waffle iron.

One thing, she had her décolleté buttoned up tight, to match her wedding ring. Like Rog said, whores make the best wives. She brought him a tissue paper full of red roses and a stack of comic books.

I tried to stand back out of the way behind the old man, but she couldn't've missed me, the color I am. She never said nothing, though. Her lipstick was painted in a smile for Roger to reach up and kiss it. Then she planted him in roses and comics and fluffed his pillow for him. The old man had his tongue out again. He slid back with his checkerboard to make room for Lulu to perch up on the bed, her fishnet legs twisted together like she was on a bar stool.

First thing Roger did was slip her purse out from under her arm, out of habit, and give it a run-through. His fingers have got fat, but he still knows how to play them— could've been a cardshark in some casino, and no more wrist motion than a curtain rod. The old man was backed up against me, so all I saw was Roger give the handbag a handjob and a fast shuffle before he shut it up again. Never saw what was in there, but Rog give me a sly wink that could've meant anything.

Then, funny thing, Roger picked up my bag of fruit and stuck it back in my hand and said to Lulu, "My friend here, my ace number one guitar player, he was just saying he has to take his fruit and hit the road."

That was my hint to say good-by, so I said it. Lulu never let on I was even alive, but Rog give me a two-finger salute, saying, "So long, ace. Eat pears, get fat and happy like me. Don't join no hillbilly bands."

Old man was the only one looked sad when I left, sorry to see the sack of fruit go with me.

I caught my same bus back to Vincennes passing up all the different hospitals full of everybody sick and weary, and passed through suburbs like suburbs anyplace—big high-rise apartment buildings going up, windowpanes whitewashed with X's so you wouldn't put your hand through them. With brand-new houses going up, naturally there was a shopping center coming in where a market-place used to be. They were sawing down the plane trees to make room for a parking lot with bushes around it planted in concrete tubs. From now on you drive in and get your TV supermarket dinner and frozen snails or a six-pack of wine without having to go to Paris anymore.

Yeah, things sliding downhill daily, but then I saw two painters painting silver paint on a kilometer of chain fence to where they was painted silver theirselves, like saints at St. Eustache—and that cheered me up again. I reached into my sack to draw me out a pear to make lunch out of it, but guess what I drew out instead. It was a hun-dred-franc note, so help me Jesus!

Twenty bucks, out of the blue. Out of Lulu's purse, rather—now I knew why Roger-D was winking at me when I went out. Didn't I tell you the man was changeable as the weather? I damn near busted out of myself with uplift. Got a notion to toss pears and cherries like a kid at all them windows with X's, for kicks. (Wait a minute, Roger-D might be moving in there next month with Lulu and their goldfish, Françoise and André next door if they missed their ship to the U.S., Marcel discharged from the army selling cheese at the new supermarket downstairs—everybody, me included, going to end up in a project or a hospital bed, they don't watch out.)

I looked at my money again and could've done a soft shoe strumming guitar right down the bus aisle. But I made myself sit still and hold it in.

William Wiser, a native of Covington, Kentucky, who divides his time between France and The Queen's University in Belfast, where he is writer-in-residence, has published stories in *Playboy, McCall's, Oui, Harper's Bazaar, TriQuarterly,* and other periodicals. He is the author of three novels: *K,* for which he received a Mary Roberts Rinehart Fellowship, *The Wolf Is Not Native to the South of France,* published in 1976, and most recently, *Disappearances.*